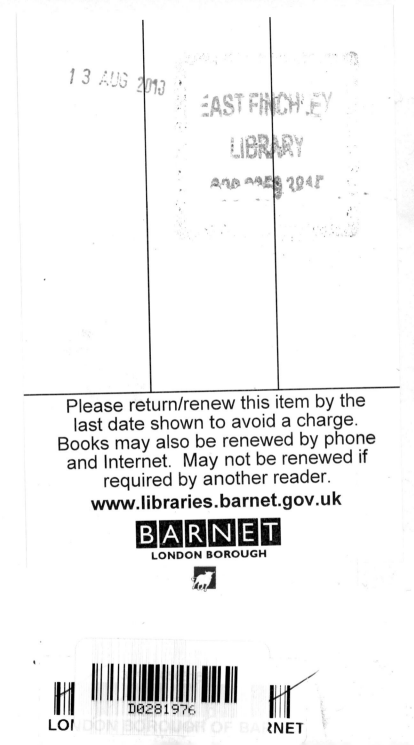

Please return/renew this item by the
last date shown to avoid a charge.
Books may also be renewed by phone
and Internet. May not be renewed if
required by another reader.
www.libraries.barnet.gov.uk

BARNET
LONDON BOROUGH

Matador
9 Priory Business Park,
Wistow Road, Kibworth Beauchamp,
Leicestershire. LE8 0RX
Tel: 0116 279 2299
Email: books@troubador.co.uk
Web: www.troubador.co.uk/matador
Twitter: @matadorbooks

ISBN 978 1788038 874

British Library Cataloguing in Publication Data.
A catalogue record for this book is available from the British Library.

Printed and bound in the UK by TJ International, Padstow, Cornwall
Typeset in 11pt Adobe Garamond Pro by Troubador Publishing Ltd, Leicester, UK

Matador is an imprint of Troubador Publishing Ltd

MIX
Paper from
responsible sources
FSC® C013056

To my mother with all my love

Bird's Milk (*Ptich'ye Moloko* in Russian)

A famous Soviet confectionary

A Slavic idiom used to describe something very precious, rare and unattainable. The phrase can be traced back to Ancient Greece where it referred to a fantastical delicacy.

"Ought one not to reject any longing for one's homeland, for any homeland besides that which is with me, within me, which is stuck like the silver sand of the sea to the skin of my soles, lives in my eyes, my blood, gives depth and distance to the background of life's every hope?"

The Gift by Vladimir Nabokov

"A rich man has everything but bird's milk"

Russian proverb

Contents

Preface

"You have to be deplorably in love with yourself to write about yourself without shame[1]," wrote Feodor Dostoevsky in his novel *The Adolescent*. When someone close to me suggested I write down the story of my journey from a Soviet child to UK citizen living and working in London, I recalled the master's words and had a moment's hesitation. But on reflection, I felt that in telling my tale, I would be helping readers get to know something I hold dear – the magnificent and often misunderstood country that is Russia.

Many Westerners I meet have a fuzzy view of Russia, often distorted by aggressive headlines published on both sides of the Atlantic. Some imagine Russia as a land of never-ending winter and wandering bears, where impoverished bearded folk survive on a diet of bread and vodka. They think of Moscow and St. Petersburg as Russia's only isles of civilisation, where fabulously wealthy oligarchs live in golden palaces (that is, when they are not partying in Monaco with their beautiful diamond-clad girlfriends).

With so many Russians now living in the US, Europe, Australia and Israel, we tend to be conspicuous. We are blunt and rather too serious, a little vain and fiercely ambitious. Most Russians appear to be hard on the outside, but once

---

1   Unless otherwise credited, all translations from Russian are my own.

you get to know us well, we are often tender and endearing. I sense that there is a great deal of interest in Russia beyond the headlines and the stereotypical stories of poverty, corruption and the super rich. What are ordinary Russians like? What are their aspirations? What do they eat? Are they really that different?

Russians living abroad won't dwell on their background beyond a couple of anecdotes and old wives' tales (for example, insisting that you eat raw garlic to cure a cold and keep your vodka in the freezer). At the same time, the media tends to entice readers with sensational events, while history and current affairs books about Russia focus on prominent personalities. This book gives my own insight into what it was like to grow up in the Soviet Union, but it also attempts to bring Russia closer to the West. After all, we live in an increasingly complicated and interconnected world of global citizens who, like me, are grappling to reconcile their roots with the new set of values they acquire on their way. It's the tale of every immigrant who suffers from a lost sense of belonging.

I was born in Sverdlovsk (now Ekaterinburg), Russia's fourth largest city. It's in the heart of the Ural Mountains, which divide Western Russia and Siberia. It takes a two-hour flight or twenty hours on a fast train to get to Ekaterinburg from Moscow. My Soviet childhood was filled with stories of Lenin, May Day demonstrations and October Revolution parades, pioneer neckerchiefs and empty shelves. The restructuring in the 1980s felt nowhere near as rapid as the newspaper headlines had suggested. Gorbachev wasn't hailed as a hero in Russia, but dismissed as a laughing stock. Still, like most Soviet citizens, we were happy, and I have only fond memories of my childhood. It's no wonder that many Russians today think of the Soviet Union with nostalgia, longing for the predictability of those carefree days when education and healthcare were free, unemployment was unheard of and the difference between the rich and the poor was a Volga, a washing machine or a state *dacha* in the Crimea – the pinnacle of Soviet aspirations.

The changes of the 1990s did not just make some individuals fabulously rich and many more devastatingly poor; they also opened up opportunities for people like me to travel beyond the borders that had constrained generations of Russians before me. We lived through colossal changes and sometimes I think we are still catching up with them. My grandfather fought the Germans in the Second World War, but when I was ten, the Berlin Wall came down and some years later I went to school in Germany. I dreamt big and applied to study in Oxford. I graduated with a degree in Economics & Management and moved to London to work in the City and then in the media, before becoming a writer.

This book is my story but it also tells a story of modern Russia. I'd like you to meet ordinary people, dive into our history, catch a glimpse of our daily lives and appreciate our values. Putin's reign has put a strain on my relationships with my family and friends in Russia. I am worried about the increasing tensions between my extraordinary native land and the West. While I struggle to reconcile Russian government actions with the liberal values by which I stand, I am equally frustrated with the 'double standards' applied to Russia in international relations. In some ways, I fear that I myself am somehow stranded in a no-man's land in the middle of it all.

This book is a journey. It began in 1986 when I was staying with my grandparents at their summer cottage.

Chapter I in which the Professor of History went mushroom picking

By the 1980s, the Soviet powerhouse began to run out of steam. No resources were spared for the defence industry, which had kept its strategic priority from the Stalin era, but the economy was struggling to look after its citizens. The Kremlin, too, was in crisis: three General Secretaries of the Soviet Politburo – Brezhnev, Andropov and Chernenko – all died in office in rapid succession.

Then, in March 1985, Mikhail Gorbachev was elected General Secretary. Most people had not heard of him previously, but he was remarked upon at once. At fifty-four, Gorbachev was considerably younger than his predecessors. His accent made him sound like a provincial bumpkin rather than a Moscow politician. Most people didn't take him seriously. But after less than a year in office, Gorbachev announced a bold set of reforms: *perestroika* (restructuring), *glasnost* (openness) and *uskoreniye* (acceleration), setting a new course to modernise and democratise the Soviet Union. For the first time in a generation, Soviet society experienced freedom of speech, political debate and an easing of state censorship.

It was the economic reforms that caused much confusion and uncertainty for the Soviet households. "Business" and "trade" weren't part of the everyday vocabulary. Soon rationing, a distant memory of the post-war days, was re-introduced due to severe shortages. In many ways, for all Gorbachev's ambitions, daily life changed very little. Still, his appointment and his reforms marked a new era, and the beginning of this story.

An old fridge at the foot of my bed shuddered and furiously burst into life. The metal wire base of the single bed, deeply concave from supporting generations of sleeping Bakunins, trembled in response. Worried I'd overslept, I bolted out of bed and pulled the curtain aside to see the day breaking. Basil the cat was crossing the yard unhurriedly, savouring the stillness of the hour. At that moment, the door of my grandparents' bedroom opened, and my grandfather, already dressed, walked through the guest room, giving me a quick nod. Careful not to wake auntie Natasha, who was sleeping in the same room (which served as a bedroom, a kitchen and a pantry) of the family *dacha*, I got up, wiping away the crumbs of a biscuit I had stolen and eaten in bed the night before. I put on my red cotton shorts and a singlet, and hurried after my grandfather. He was already outside, refilling a small tank with fresh water from the well. We used an aluminium container with a manual plunger, fixed to a fence, to wash our hands and splash the slumber away. I ran to the toilet. It was a simple wooden structure, but with a dollop of imagination it resembled the first Soviet spacecraft sent into space, and so we affectionately called it "Vostok 1".

"I'm ready!" I beamed. I was six and both happy and apprehensive about my grandfather taking me mushroom picking with him for the very first time.

My grandfather, *Deda* Sasha or *Dedushka*, wore sturdy trousers, a long-sleeved shirt, a wide-brimmed hat and galoshes, perfect for walking through the dew-drenched grass. He looked me over from head to toe.

"The mosquitos will have you for breakfast," he said at last.

Anxious not to keep him waiting, I shrugged and smiled. Dedushka handed me a small woven basket and a knife, and we headed for the forest.

***

Aleksandr (Sasha) Bakunin was my paternal grandfather. He was born in 1924 in a village called Tundrino in the Tumen region of Western Siberia. He was the youngest of four children in a peasant family, living off the land. The family worked in a *kolkhoz*, a Soviet collective farm. When the Bolsheviks had abolished private ownership of land after the October Revolution of 1917, they established large collective farms on which peasants were employed to grow crops. These were then distributed centrally rather than through market forces. Families still supported themselves with fishing, hunting and foraging, but trade was illegal, even if the so-called black markets were ubiquitous. Aleksandr finished school and left home for a teacher training college in Tobolsk, an old town in the same region some 500km away. In 1942, when he turned eighteen, he was conscripted into the Red Army and followed his elder brothers, already fighting the Nazis on the fronts in Western Russia and Ukraine. Thanks to his education, Aleksandr was singled out and tasked with teaching new recruits in Kuybyshev (now Samara) on the east bank of the river Volga. After the war, he returned to Western Siberia and got a job in a village school, as did his brother Ivan. Aleksandr's eldest brother Mikhail, who had fought to liberate Kiev, married and settled down in Ukraine.

The war years changed Aleksandr, for the boundaries of his world had expanded far beyond the Siberian plain. Working as a schoolteacher in an isolated provincial village proved uninspiring. He aimed higher and dreamt of going to university. In summer 1947, Aleksandr travelled to Sverdlovsk (now Ekaterinburg), an industrial and cultural hub in the heart of the Ural Mountains. His ambition was to study history. Wearing army trousers and tall leather boots, Aleksandr turned up at the admissions commission of the Ural State University (now part of the merged Ural Federal University, UrFU). He handed in his papers to an earnest-looking brunette sitting in front of two neat piles of applications. He thought the image of a defender of the Motherland would help secure him a place as a mature student. The brunette was called Lena after the great Russian river which flows from Lake Baikal into the Arctic ocean. She was a chemistry student working as an admissions secretary over the summer, and was under strict instructions to reject all hopefuls who did not already have accommodation in Sverdlovsk – the student dorms were all full. Unimpressed with Aleksandr's bravado, or his unrefined *sibiryak* (native Siberian) looks, she promptly rejected his application, explaining the accommodation situation in her clear, unmistakeable city accent.

This was how my grandparents met. Aleksandr refused to take 'no' for an answer, rented a room in an old wooden house together with three other students and persuaded the head of admissions to give him a place. My grandmother Lena never forgot the triumphant look on the stubborn *sibiryak*'s face, when he came back with the papers. Two years later he asked Lena to marry him. They moved into Lena's parents' home: a small flat, heated by a wood stove. Aleksandr passed his exams with distinction and, like all Soviet graduates, was assigned a job: in his case, an academic post at the department of Marxism-Leninism at the history faculty of the Ural State Technical University (now part of UrFU). Lena worked at the chemistry faculty of the same university.

Specialising in the industrial development of the Urals in the 1930s, my grandfather got his doctorate and then became a professor of history, heading up the prestigious Department of History of the Communist Party of the Soviet Union at the Ural State Technical University. During his academic career, he supervised over ninety doctoral students and published nearly 400 papers and books.

In early 1960s the regional government granted land to Sverdlovsk academics for their recreational use in the summer. Each family got six *sotki* or 600 square metres (just under 6,500 square feet), permission to build a simple summer cottage (at their own expense) and to plant apple trees, but not potatoes. (Apparently, while fruit trees were conducive to relaxation from academic work, potatoes were considered as a crop, which ought to be grown in the *kolkhoz*.) My grandparents were assigned an allotment in a place called Flyus, 40km from Sverdlovsk, right in the middle of forest and within walking distance of a large freshwater reservoir, Volchikhinskoye.

Dedushka laid the foundations and built a one-storey house with his own bare hands. He also constructed a brick wood-burning stove for heating and cooking. The house had a single proper bedroom assigned to my grandparents and everyone else settled either in a guestroom by the stove or in a busy veranda, where we ate and prepared food, washed the dishes and sheltered from the rain. Baba Lena planted not only apple trees but also raspberry, gooseberry, redcurrant and blackcurrant bushes, strawberries, vegetables and herbs. The *dachas* might have been decreed places of recreation, but in practice the academics developed their allotments for their livelihood. As soon as the snow had melted by the end of April, my grandfather would drive his beloved Volga to Flyus to tend the garden, impatient to move there for the summer. Every year, up until my teens, I stayed at the family *dacha* for a month at a time.

***

Dedushka and I turned towards a birch grove. He kept himself to himself, walking with the confidence of someone with an intimate knowledge of the forest. It was as if each aspen tree, every moss-covered stump, were landmarks on a carefully drawn map. I was so conscious of the honour of picking mushrooms with my grandfather that I too kept quiet, hoping to spot a *podosinovik* or a *podberezovik*.

Mushroom picking is a bit like playing chess: it's all very well to move a pawn or spot a *syroezhka* (also *sinyavka* – a russule, a common edible mushroom), but it's the royalty that really counts. Mushroom royalty are *belye* (literally – white mushrooms; ceps, penny buns or porcini), followed by *podosinoviks* or *krasnogoloviks* (literally – mushrooms that grow under aspen trees or mushrooms with red heads) and *podberezoviks* (literally – mushrooms that grow under birch trees). These prized fare hide under fallen leaves and behind tussocks. By contrast, *syroezhki* are easy to come by. So, however, are *poganki* – inedible, poisonous mushrooms, which look deceptively like the good ones. Dedushka was a brilliant chess player, and always came back from the forest with a basket full of ceps.

The birch grove was sparkling with dew and animated by birdsong. Soon I began chirping even louder than the birds.

"Is this a good one, Dedushka?" I asked hopefully.

"It's *poganka*," he replied, glancing briefly at the impostor I had spotted.

"And what about that one?" I asked, desperate to get it right.

"*Sinyavka!*" His tone of voice indicated that a common mushroom was as much of a disappointment as an inedible one.

After a while, my grandfather stopped to sit on a stump to smoke a *papirosa*, a strong cigarette without a filter. His blue eyes appeared half closed, as if focussed on a distant memory of some Siberian forest. Unable to sit still, I decided to look for wild strawberries. Whether you are six or sixty, finding these tiny, delicate, impossibly sweet treasures is always a joy. I came back with a handful of garnets, glowing with pride. Dedushka took some from my palm, smiling. I was beaming for the rest of the outing, oblivious to the mosquitos, which, as my grandfather had predicted, were feasting off me.

Once we had filled both our baskets, my only *krasnogolovik* placed strategically on top of my pile, we returned to the *dacha*. My grandmother served breakfast on a long wooden table on the veranda: *tvorog* (cottage cheese or quark) with tangy sour cream, topped with raspberries and gooseberries from the garden. Black tea and fresh blackcurrant leaves sat brewing in a chipped, stained pot with a faded pattern of forget-me-nots.

Baba Lena looked impeccable as usual. Her hair was dyed chestnut red and carefully permed. Even in the country, she slept lying on her front, with her forehead on her forearm in order to preserve her coiffure. Born in Sverdlovsk, Baba Lena had had an urban upbringing, which made her not exactly proud but certainly poised. While my other grandmother took me to the circus, Baba Lena bought me season tickets to the ballet when I was about nine or ten. She loved her *dacha* for its flair, vaguely reminiscent of the countryside setting of the stories by Chekhov, Bunin and Kuprin she read at bedtime.

After breakfast, I helped Baba Lena to sort and wash our harvest while Basil the cat stretched in the sun, showing off his stripy grey belly. My grandmother set some mushrooms aside to pan-fry for dinner, but the bulk of the crop was to be preserved for the winter.

"With Gorbachev running the country, you don't know what to expect," she said to no one in particular.

She quickly prepped the mushrooms I had washed. My *krasnogolovik* too met its communist fate, its royal roots notwithstanding: its head was chopped off, sliced, seasoned and put into a jar with the rest of the crop for the greater common good.

During the summer months, the professor hardly ever sat still. He spent his days outside, fishing at dawn, picking mushrooms and berries, entirely in his element. He would rise at six every morning and keep busy until lunchtime. He chopped wood, dug vegetable patches and planted trees. He even made me a swing, which became a favourite attraction among the children from neighbouring *dachas*. Only when the summer rains arrived unannounced and stayed, like an uninvited guest, dampening the mood, did Dedushka come indoors. He would often bring his trusted friend Tibor the Pekingese with him and attempt to brush his tangled black-and-white coat. Neither the dog nor the master enjoyed it, and both were impatient to be outdoors again.

His eldest daughter Natalya must have inherited her father's inability to sit still. She too was fond of the *dacha* and spent the entire summer working in the garden. Auntie Natasha, as I called her, was four years older than my father and taught technical drawing at a university. In contrast to the precise nature of drafting when she was at work, the *dacha*'s garden was her creative pasture. She grew purple asters, orange marigolds, scarlet gladioli and fuchsia-coloured dahlias. Auntie Natasha was most frequently found bottom up, wearing red lipstick and gloves (to protect her manicure), weeding and singing. She was particularly fond of the nation's favourite, Alla Pugacheva, and her hit song *One Million Roses*. Auntie Natasha's only son Dima (my first cousin and seven years my senior) was entirely indifferent to his mother's passions: experimental cooking and strawberry face masks. Sadly, I preferred eating strawberries to smearing them all over my face, but I did enjoy her culinary tours of the garden.

"Yanka, did you know that poached rhubarb tastes great with thick sour cream?" she would ask, imitating a TV presenter, "And sea-buckthorn berry can be used to make a refreshing sweet-and-sour drink," she'd continue in her sing-song voice. If she spotted her beloved Basil sampling a mint leaf or napping under a shrub, auntie Natasha would interrupt the garden show to shower her cat with a wealth of elaborate diminutives, of which only the Russian language can boast. I myself was only ever called by my proper name "Yana", when I was being disciplined; otherwise my family and friends called me "Yanka", "Yassya", "Yass'ka", "Yanulya", "Yanochka", "Yassen'ka", "Yanych", "Yanchik", "Yanok" or "Yanische". While auntie Natasha was not looking, I would pull a carrot, wash it in a barrel filled with rainwater and munch away. I was always feeling peckish.

***

In the middle of the summer we ate the same thing every lunchtime: a bowl of *okroshka*. First soup bowls were filled with diced cucumbers, radishes, cooked potatoes, eggs and leftover cooked meat or ham, chopped spring onions and dill, mixed together and seasoned, then *kvas* was poured over the 'salad' and the 'soup' was garnished with sour cream. *Kvas* is a fermented non-alcoholic drink made from rye bread. My grandmother always made her own *kvas*, which was chilled in large glass jars in the cold spring, next to a fresh water well that my grandfather had dug back when they had been assigned their piece of land for the *dacha*. Auntie Natasha would add some strong mustard to her *okroshka*, as she always liked to 'improve' her dishes with an extra ingredient. While her parents, who had lived through the war, ate everything with a couple of slices of bread, she preferred swapping bread for a mighty bunch of lovage, spring onion and wild garlic.

To the crunch of greens and the slurps of *okroshka*, the

conversation that summer centred around *glasnost*. Auntie Natasha fantasised about travelling abroad. The word *zagranitsa* (abroad) was always rolled off the tongue with a sense of promise and a hint of mystery. Auntie Natasha dreamt of a denim jacket. I was not sure what denim was, but my grandfather wasn't impressed. He raised one eyebrow in silent disapproval. His own hope for *glasnost* was that perhaps he could now gain access to historic documents, banned and buried away by a succession of Soviet governments.

Dedushka told us about the Ipatiev House, a historic building in Sverdlovsk, where he had worked to research his PhD. The Ipatiev House used to be a merchant's mansion in the centre of Ekaterinburg (before the city was named Sverdlovsk after Yakov Sverdlov, a prominent Bolshevik). It had housed the family of the last Russian tsar, Nikolai II, who was kept in exile there following his abdication in 1918 after the Bolshevik Revolution. Nikolai Romanov, his wife, their four daughters, their son and their servants, lived in the house for over two months, isolated from the outside world. In July 1918, the family was woken up in the middle of the night and instructed to get dressed and assemble down in the basement, ready to be moved to a new location. Downstairs they were told that their relatives and supporters had attempted to rescue them, which could jeopardise the Bolsheviks' impending victory. The family was read the execution order and the shots followed. Some bullets ricocheted off the jewels hidden in the princesses' corsets. The executioners had to finish the job with bayonets.

The bodies were buried down an abandoned mine pit 15km north of Ekaterinburg. The Soviets later made every effort to erase all memory of the imperial family from the Ipatiev House, converting it into a State Communist Party archive. My grandfather spent a lot of time in that archive, working on his doctorate on the history of the Urals, reviewing censored documents, limited to what suited the official party line. As the place where the last Russian tsar met his fate, the Ipatiev House continued to attract pilgrims, and so the Soviet government eventually decided to demolish the building in 1977 and invaluable historic documents disappeared within the vast bureaucracy of the Soviet machine.

***

At the end of a hot day, auntie Natasha always took me swimming at the Volchikhinskoe reservoir. She too was glad to wash away the mosquito repellent and stretch after a day of kneeling over radishes. That summer I remember swimming with a blue inflatable ring, which was a present from Dedushka. He had gone to a conference in Moscow on the history of the Communist Party of the Soviet Union. It was obviously a momentous occasion; the entire family wrote him a shopping list for Moscow's GUM, the main department store, which was regarded as the atheist equivalent of the Holy Grail. The GUM sold toys and clothes, food and kitchenware, spare parts for sewing machines and stationery. Moscow shops offered *choice*. Grandfather came back with my swimming ring and a suitcase of presents for each of his children and their families.

In those days, a trip to Moscow was invariably associated with a pound of decent *kolbasa* (ham or sausage) and a bag of the finest chocolates. The chocolate factories Babaev, Red October and Rotfront made the best chocolate in the entire Soviet Union or, as I saw it, the world. Each variety was a fairy tale in itself, with names such as Mishki v Lesu (Little Bears in the Forest), Mishki na Severe (Little Bears in the North), Mishka Kosolapy (Pigeon-toed Little Bear), Metelitsa (a Russian name for the German fairy tale Mother Hulda) and Burevestnik (Thunderbird). Every chocolate was beautifully wrapped in foil and colourful paper. The Bakunin family loved their chocolate, but trips to Moscow were, unfortunately, rare.

The Volchikhinskoe reservoir was named after a nearby mountain, Volchikha (She-wolf), draped in evergreen fir trees. It was formed in 1944 by the building of a dam on the river Chusovaya to supply water to Sverdlovsk. The reservoir is so vast that it's simply referred to as "the lake". I walked down the slope to the water and plunged in, fearless thanks to my ring. Auntie Natasha was conscious of her perm and swam with her head held high. In the late afternoon, some fishermen would come by with their angling rods and worms to try their luck at catching bream or perch. Dedushka often took his boat out as well. He loved a fishing expedition and got his friends together both in summer and in winter (when the thick layer of ice on the lake had to be drilled through to reach the fish below).

Sometimes after swimming, auntie Natasha and I would go to meet uncle Borya, Natasha's husband, who would arrive from Sverdlovsk on a local train. The station – a ticket booth with a couple of benches in a waiting room – was right by the lake. Uncle Borya was a fellow of the Theory of Communism department of the philosophy faculty at the Ural State University. Typically, he wore dark-rimmed glasses, a chequered shirt, a brown suit and a flat cap and carried a worn leather briefcase, as he would come straight from work. Inevitably, he would also bring a shopping net bulging with packets of sugar for making jam and bottles of vinegar for preserving mushrooms and cucumbers. There would be a pile of newspapers under his arm – *Pravda*, *Argumenty i Fakty* and *Izvestia* (*Truth*, *Arguments* and *Facts and News*) – to share the latest press with his parents-in-law.

Uncle Borya was reserved compared to our family of openly opinionated academics. Perhaps it was simply his way of respecting his in-laws. At university he was well regarded and liked. I remember visiting him at his office years later: he was chain-smoking at his desk, surrounded by volumes of leather-bound books. His colleagues and students popped in unceremoniously, sank into the black leather sofa next to me for a spell, and asked him for advice or a cigarette, before running off. Uncle Borya taught politics but never voted. He ate little but smoked a lot. He read thick books but ignored newspapers. Uncle Borya was our 'house philosopher', and I thought he was exceptionally clever. But he was never patronising to me and often invited me for "a conversation" on a makeshift bench in front of the cottage. One time I sang him a song I had learned in kindergarten about our Motherland. I was especially enthusiastic about the last couplet:

> *I do not know any other country like this,*
> *Where a man can breathe with so much ease!*

Uncle Borya frowned all of a sudden and said: "I don't know any other country either, but that's because very few Soviet citizens are allowed to travel abroad."

My beloved blue ring inspired me to tell Uncle Borya my guilty secret. When my kindergarten teacher had asked me about my favourite colour, I reckoned it was blue. The teacher explained to me patiently that my favourite colour ought to be red, like the Soviet flag. I felt ashamed and asked Uncle Borya for advice.

"Blue is a lovely colour, I am glad it's your favourite," said my uncle, his brown eyes twinkling behind his glasses.

It pleased me so much I remember skipping all the way back to the *dacha*.

***

At dinner grandfather always sat at the head of the table; the other adults sat on a long bench facing the window of the veranda and I sat at the opposite end of the table, sharing it with my cousin, if he was around. The food was prepared in the same room, cooked either on a small electric cooker or on the wood stove in the anteroom. Auntie Natasha liked to cut a bunch of asters to decorate the table. Baba Lena often made me a drink with squashed sour sea-buckthorn berries. Uncle Borya brought a bottle of vodka. Grandfather liked to have a shot of vodka, sometimes two, despite his wife's protests.

For dinner I liked *golubtsy*, which were cabbage rolls, also known as pigs in a blanket: cooked minced meat bulked up with rice, wrapped in cabbage leaves and simmered in a pot. As a treat Baba Lena often served sunflower seed *khalva*, a

Middle Eastern delicacy that looked like pieces of grey rock, with *kefir*, a little sour fermented dairy drink. I always sat eating quiet as a mouse, absorbed in the adult conversation. Uncle Borya and grandfather talked about Gorbachev's reforms. Dedushka seemed so affected by the draft of change that he shivered a little after his shot of vodka. Uncle Borya wondered whether the new General Secretary had enough power to see through any real change. However ambitious Gorbachev might appear with his big ideas of *glasnost* and *perestroika*, it was a different matter entirely to break through the tightly cemented foundations of the Central Committee of the Party. Most of the Central Committee members who served under Brezhnev during the times of *zastoy* (stagnation) were old and entirely opposed to change, especially if proposals were at odds with the Communist doctrine. An individual reformer was powerless, whereas the Party's influence was ubiquitous: every job, especially an academic position, was dependent on it. Uncle Borya, for example, was hoping to become the head of the philosophy faculty one day. If he embraced Gorbachev's political thaw openly, the local Party cadres were likely to disapprove and even overlook his promotion, on the basis of a lack of "ideological maturity".

Uncle Borya fetched water from the spring and Baba Lena boiled it in a kettle on the wood stove so I could wash the dishes. I tried hard not to clatter the plates so that I could still listen to the conversation behind me. It did not occur to me that adults could feel as confused as I did about the future or the past. We were all born and bred in the Soviet Union, the country which had sent the first man into space, which prided itself on its free education and healthcare for all, its

Nobel Prizes in physics and advances in medicine, its sports and the 1980 Moscow Olympics, and its superior ideology. I knew that in the Soviet Union people were equal and happy, sharing and enjoying our country's vast nationalised resources, unlike in the West, where poor workers were exploited by capitalists and had to pay dearly for housing, water, university education and healthcare. It was unthinkable to question Communism, especially for a six-year-old hoping to start school in September and, more pressingly, dying to get another chocolate or at least a toffee. When the dishes were done, it was time for the nightly ritual of making the open fire.

After dinner, my grandfather liked to go outside to savour the remainder of the day, sitting by the fire in front of the cottage, smoking a *papirosa* and patting Tibosha, as we called Tibor affectionately. The dog was well aware of his superior status as grandfather's best friend and wasn't overly friendly towards me, a young upstart, born some years after him. Tibosha trotted to his master, following him around faithfully as Dedushka kindled the fire from a small pile of chippings and a page from an old *Pravda*. Grandfather used to send me to get more firewood from the forest as he sat down on a large round log, his companion beside him. I would sprint to the woods looking for dry twigs and pine bark, gathering an armful and returning, impatient to settle down next to Dedushka.

There we would sit, as the flames nibbled hungrily at the wood, devouring the logs and from time to time belching sparks of light. Mosquitos began their nightly concert, their violins sadly out of tune. The dog would let out a deep sigh, perfectly synchronised with his master's. What was the professor thinking about? Could he foresee the unravelling of the Soviet Union, like a bright flame eventually reducing to a pile of shimmering coals?

Chapter II in which my father built a girl

In the West, Gorbachev became a celebrity. The new Soviet leader travelled abroad, shook hands with Western politicians and even smiled for the camera. In 1986 he met with the US President Ronald Reagan and proposed to ban all ballistic missiles. Their talks collapsed, but a year later the USSR and the USA signed a treaty which put a brake on the arms race. It was, perhaps, Gorbachev's most important political legacy.

The Soviet General Secretary got on famously well with the British Prime Minister Margaret Thatcher. She once said: "I like Mr Gorbachev, we can do business together."

In the Soviet Union people told incessant jokes about Gorbachev and ridiculed his laws, his accent and his birthmark. Thatcher, on the other hand, won Russian hearts. Her interview on the Soviet television[1] lasted forty-five minutes and was broadcast in full, which was unprecedented for an appearance of a capitalist leader on Soviet mass media. It was from Thatcher that Russians learned about the scale of the Soviet nuclear arsenal. She also talked about ordinary things like her typical breakfast and lunch. The contrast between her and the detached Soviet general secretaries was striking. Still, as the "Iron Lady", Thatcher was everything Russians admired in a leader: strong, charismatic, patriotic and decisive.

Sverdlovsk and Divnomorsk, summer 1986

I was born in 1979, the same year Margaret Thatcher became

---

1   On 31 March 1987

Prime Minister of the United Kingdom, a political event that caused ripples well beyond the British Isles. The Iron Lady appeared to be a superwoman: a head of state, a wife and a mother. My father felt inspired.

"And don't take the lift on your way back up!" he shouted after me, as I tumbled out of our flat to begin my compulsory Saturday morning run.

His instruction was clear: two loops. Skipping down six flights of stairs, I comforted myself with the thought that mum was mixing batter for pancakes, my favourite weekend breakfast.

Our square yard was surrounded by four blocks of flats that had been built in the 1970s in the typical Soviet style. I started running alongside one of the blocks, a grey nine-storey building, housing 144 flats. Every flat on Onufriev Street, which was named after a distinguished revolutionary, had the same layout: a kitchen, a living room, a bathroom, a toilet and either one or two bedrooms. The planners designed the flats to have balconies, facing away from the communal yard. We had a view of a motorway; our neighbours faced an orphanage. The balconies were intended for leisure (a game of chess on a sunny afternoon, perhaps), but in reality were used for storage. Ours was packed with homemade pickled mushrooms and other vegetables, a variety of garden berry jams, sacks of potatoes, three sets of cross country skis, a wash tub and my father's hunting gear.

The block opposite ours had its entrances facing the other way. A row of poplar trees and acacia bushes had been planted alongside that building. They concealed a path beyond the watchful eye of my father, who was observing me from the window. As soon as I reached the welcome refuge, I slowed to a walk. From behind the foliage I could see other children already filling the playground, building sand castles, taking turns on a swing or at skipping. Sighing, I moved up a gear as I reached the end of the tree line. I trotted over my own chalk drawings left over from yesterday's game of hopscotch. Each side of the yard was about 150m long, every bit as torturous as the last. I was four and a half when my father first sent me running one summer Saturday morning. It became a regular practice. I hated running, I hated being watched by hundreds of windows, some open on a warm morning, with lace curtains lured outside by the draft. One loop done, one to go.

Finally, my ordeal was over. Climbing up the stairs, I bumped into our neighbours from the second floor, taking their Newfoundland Styepa out for a walk. It was not uncommon to keep St. Bernard's, Great Danes and Newfoundlands in cramped Soviet flats. Styepa blocked my way with his enormous black frame and was drooling in anticipation of his walk. Back at home, the kitchen door was closed to prevent smoke from the gas stove travelling through the flat. I could see mum through the frosted glass, spreading clarified butter onto the cast iron pan, pouring batter in a delicately thin layer, then flipping it over with the tips of her fingers. If she did not have enough batter for a full pancake at the end, she fried it anyway and let me scoff a hot, yummy scrap before breakfast. Tummy singing, I went to my room. My father was determined that I should not let my gymnastics practice get rusty during the summer break. Getting down into a split, I was wondering which jam mum would be opening for the pancakes: blueberry or raspberry?

Most Soviet citizens lived in flats that were granted to them by the State via professional unions to which they belonged. State enterprises put their employees on a waiting list for a new 'state' flat, but a new home required ten to twenty years of patience. In 1958 a Soviet decree laid the foundations for the so-called 'co-operative' tower blocks, newly built properties with flats for sale at the prices determined by the State, which based their valuation on the costs of construction and internal decoration. While one could join a queue and eventually buy a flat from a 'co-operative', it was not possible to sell it until the privatisation reform of the early 1990s. A typical classified ad in the days of the Soviet Union might offer to exchange a two-bedroom flat for a one-bedroom flat and a studio, following a divorce, for example.

A university lecturer and an engineer could not afford to buy a flat outright or even make the first instalment. When my parents got married, their parents put their savings together and bought them a newly built two-bedroom flat and furniture. The kitchen was small, so we had weekend breakfast in the living room. Here wooden cabinets, finished to resemble mahogany, displayed hardcover collections of the full works of Pushkin, Lermontov, Chekhov and other Russian classics. Underneath the bookshelves, crystalware was on display in a glass cabinet, as was the convention. Even a modest family drank Georgian wines and Russian vodka from crystal glasses. A second dining set and silverware, reserved for special occasions, were hidden inside the drawers below. The cabinet's glass doors reflected an ABBA poster, hanging on the opposite wall. There was a mustard-coloured carpet on the floor with a Persian design but a Soviet thread. A black-and-white television set stood next to a record player.

Whenever I was ill and could not go to kindergarten, and later school, my mum stayed home with me. She made me a nest of pillows, cushions and blankets on the living room sofa and put on an LP. We had quite a collection of children's fairy tales and musicals, my favourite of which was *The Town Musicians of Bremen*. It was an animated musical, loosely based on a folktale recorded by the Brothers Grimm. The Soviet version, released as a cartoon and an LP in 1969, told of a donkey, a dog, a cat, a rooster and a troubadour, who travel and sing together. One day they arrive at a palace where a widowed king lives with his beautiful daughter. The princess and the troubadour fall in love and run away, embracing freedom, friendship and life outdoors. A staggering twenty-eight million copies of *The Town Musicians of Bremen* LP were sold in the Soviet Union within two years of its release. Despite the success, its director, Inessa Kovalevskaya, was widely criticised. Her princess wore a mini skirt; her troubadour was clad in flared trousers; the donkey had bleached hair under his unmistakably Adidas cap; and the troupe played 'imported' electric guitars. The lyrics also sounded a little too liberal for the Ministry of Culture's liking. Kovalevskaya was accused of corrupting Soviet children with the hippie culture of the West and was reportedly denied membership of the cinematographic union because of her lack of professionalism. Unaware that I was lapping up Western propaganda along with mum's chicken broth, I sang along:

What are today's children like
It's impossible to rule them
We spend our health on them
But they do not care

Mum did not mind and nor did Ludmila Sergeevna, a state paediatrician who visited all the local children when they fell ill. She probably expressed some concern over me bellowing with a sore throat, but her son, too, loved children's LPs. Ludmila Sergeevna had the very same record player at home.

***

Pancake breakfast was a ritual. Like French crêpes, traditional Russian pancakes or *bliny* are the size of a dinner plate. I would fold a pancake in half, put a dollop of sour cream and a spoonful of preserved raspberries on top, then fold it again and pick it up with my hands before biting into the sweet and messy indulgence. My mother's *bliny* were delicately thin and soft. Her own mother made them thin and crispy. Her mother-in-law's pancakes were thick and fluffy from added yeast. Every Russian family has a pet feud over a traditional recipe, but my allegiance never faltered: mum's *bliny* were the best and I would stuff myself every time she made them.

I cannot help but remember my mother as she looked in those days, with her beautifully permed, silky black hair and her oversized round glasses with a touch of flour on the frames. Tall, always elegantly dressed and perfectly made-up, she was the dashing brunette of Teploproekt, the state construction planning institute, where she worked as an engineer. As a child, I was not particularly inspired by her technical drawings of industrial ovens when I visited her open-plan office, but I always thought she looked beautiful – with or without mascara.

Sometimes after breakfast mum would send me to Universam, a 'universal store'. I was given a tiny yellow coupon for butter, some coins and a net of milk and lemonade bottles to return to the recycling store. Recycling was an integral part of Soviet culture. A few times a year, after school, children were organised to collect scrap metal from neighbouring yards as part of the collective effort for the greater good. At home, we saved up old newspapers and magazines because for every 20kg of recycled paper one could get a coupon for a newly printed hardback edition of *The Three Musketeers*. We also recycled lemonade, wine, beer and dairy bottles in exchange for a refund. Even as a six-year-old, I was delighted to earn some pocket money and I always had plans as to how to spend it. The recycling store smelled of sour milk and something fermented and sticky. As soon as I got my *kopeikas*, I ran to Universam, past the yellow *kvas* booth, past the pigeons who were greedily gobbling up millet grains someone had scattered for them, and past the row of private vendors with their illicit market stalls. They were mostly old women with scarves on their heads and hands stained by the berries they had picked at dawn to bring fresh to market. Their thick bunches of spring onions and dill, perfectly ripe tomatoes, strawberries and blueberries, sold by the bucket, mocked the modest selection of groceries available inside the state store. At the entrance there was an automated dispenser of soda water and syrup. Soviet lemonade was immortalised by

Mikhail Bulgakov in *The Master and Margarita* where in the very first scene of the novel, on a hot day, the chairman of the Moscow literary association and a poet end up drinking warm lemonade in the absence of cold beer or sparkling mineral water: "The apricot lemonade came with an abundance of yellow foam, and the air began to smell of the hairdresser's." I inserted three *kopeikas* into a slot, which produced first a loud burp, then a glass of the geyser-fizzy golden drink. As a responsible citizen, I always rinsed the glass for the next thirsty customer.

In 1986 shopping was a task made easy without the distractions of choice. I would hand in my coupon at the cold counter to get a slab of butter. It was wrapped in white paper with BUTTER written across it in green letters. Eggs were sold in open carton trays or wrapped in crude paper parcels. Sour cream, milk and *kefir* were poured into glass jars and sealed with shiny foil caps with emerald, blue or purple stripes to tell them apart. Another staple was a wobbly plastic pot of mayonnaise "Provençal", pronounced in the French manner. It sounded terribly opulent and exotic, whereas, in fact, it was a common sauce we used to dress any salad or pour over roast potatoes. The final item on mum's list, written in her curvy handwriting on a piece of squared paper, was always "bread". This was not quite as straightforward as it sounds, for there was a choice between white bread (also known as a 'brick' for its shape), a round light rye loaf, a dark sourdough rye bread with coriander and caraway seeds on top (the famous "Borodinskiy") and a baguette, which had been so thoroughly sovietised that no Frenchman would have been able to trace its genetic origin. I remember once loitering at the counter and eavesdropping on a conversation between two women complaining to one another that no fresh bread had been delivered that day.

"It's that Gorbachev character with an ink splash on his head and his ideas!" complained one woman, sizing up a rye loaf.

"That's it – it's him and his *perestroika*!" echoed another.

Quite unexpectedly she broke into a *chastushka*, a traditional humorous Russian folk song, consisting of a four-lined couplet, often accompanied by a *balalaika* (accordion):

> *We don't drink vodka no more*
> *We don't eat sugar galore*
> *We now brush teeth with bricks*
> *And listen to Gorbachev's tricks.*

I grabbed a loaf of Borodinskiy because my father liked it, and hurried to the tills. I was not concerned with bread or vodka but what would become of my beloved ice cream.

Outside Universam there was a small kiosk with a promising sign: "Ice Cream". While I had heard romantic stories about "Eskimo", a mysterious brand of ice cream *covered in chocolate* and sold on a stick in the far-away land that was Moscow, in my own experience ice cream came in three varieties: "Milk" which cost ten *kopeika*, "Cream" which cost fifteen *kopeika*, and "Plombir" for eighteen *kopeika*. The latter variety was impossibly creamy, presumably just like the French classic *Glace Plombières*, described by Honoré de Balzac in *The Splendours and Miseries of Courtesans*. All three varieties were sold in soggy waffle cones and tasted vaguely of vanilla. Sometimes when I had earned some pocket money from recycling, I would ask for Plombir and lick it all the way home.

***

In the middle of summer 1986 when I would ordinarily be staying with my grandparents at the *dacha*, I was summoned back to Sverdlovsk by my father. I was to sit a school entrance exam, the most significant event in my life! There were plenty of schools spread around Sverdlovsk; they were all free and children were usually allocated to the nearest school in their neighbourhood. The schools had no names, just numbers, (we lived near school No. 159), perhaps to enforce the idea of their uniformity. In practice, of course, some schools were better than others. The best-regarded schools in Sverdlovsk were No. 9 (known for its intensive tuition in physics and maths), No. 37, which specialised in German as a foreign language, No. 39, which specialised in French, and schools No. 2, 13 and 70, which focussed on English. In those schools English was taught from the very first year, so that pupils learned to read and write in Russian and English simultaneously. My father wanted me to be one of those pupils. His ambition for me was to get a good education at a prestigious Sverdlovsk school. It so happened that school No. 70 was closest to where we lived and on the way to my parents' work.

This grand plan was, however, undermined by a number of significant obstacles. Firstly, I was too young. Children had to turn seven before the 1st of September, the start of the new academic year in every Soviet school. On paper, I was not eligible to apply, because I was not going to turn seven until December. Secondly, there was the small matter of the entrance exam itself.

My grandparents were friends with another academic family who had built their *dacha* in Flyus. Their son Zhora and my father were childhood friends. Zhora's wife Tatiana knew someone in the administration of school No. 70. Tatiana always looked very striking, especially when she came over to our *dacha* one weekend with her neatly blow-dried bob, which seemed outlandish in the rural setting. Exhaling a ring of smoke from her cigarette, Tatiana said:

"*Semidesyatka* (nickname formed from the word "seventy") favours applicants who live nearby, that's the rule. Still, if she does well in her entrance exam, they'll overlook her postcode *and* her age. Can she read?"

Mum was reluctant to send me to school early, but she nodded with the confidence only wounded pride can produce.

"Of course she can."

"Teach her some maths too and a bit of English", Tatiana continued.

"*How do you do?*" said mum, fastidiously mimicking a British accent.

They laughed and finished their cigarettes in silence, while I mimed the strange words, as unsavoury in their foreignness as the smell of tobacco.

Over the summer weekends my father explained addition and subtraction to me, and we practised reading. He even tried to teach me some English pronunciation. Sadly, his "th" in "then" sounded like "z" in "Zen" and "th" in "thin" sounded like "s" in "sin". The English "r" seemed to me deeply ironic, given that my mum had been taking me to a speech therapist to learn how to roll the Russian "r" and now I'd have to learn to tone it down again, *if I got in.*

On the day of the exam my father and I took a trolley-bus to March 8th Street, its name celebrating International Women's Day and all female revolutionaries. Of course, Sverdlovsk had a Rosa Luxembourg Street and a Clara Tsetkin Street too. The school on March 8th Street housed a three-storey nineteenth-century building with dandelion yellow walls and white ornaments around its windows. The building was empty save for a string of pre-school children and their parents, clinging to the walls of the ground floor corridor like bindweed. One classroom was clearly the lions' den: terrified boys and girls were periodically summoned to come inside and then reappeared looking either very pale or red as beetroot. A lady with a large coiffure and glasses sliding down her nose appeared to be registering hopeful applicants.

"Boy, what is your name?" she asked not unkindly.

I had worn my best clothes: red tartan dungarees that mum's sister had bought me in Moscow, and my hair was cut short, just as my father had insisted.

"My name is Yana Bakunina and I am a *girl*", I said in a small voice.

Inside a large classroom, which appeared to be a music room with a piano positioned by the window, I was passed from one imposing teacher to another. They asked me to read from a story about young Lenin, and then do simple sums. The third examiner was a woman with heavily underlined eyes and thick-rimmed butterfly-shaped glasses. She leaned close to me and asked me to repeat after her: "Ship, sheep; ship, sheep". Her lips exaggerated the long "ee", revealing a set of big white teeth. There were black bits in the corners of her eyes from the caked eyeliner. I repeated after her, my voice trailing off, as she leaned so close to me that I feared her glasses might fall off her nose. Finally, she turned aside to write something in her notebook. Taking a chance to look around, I spotted a familiar-looking woman quizzing another candidate. I realised that I had seen her the other day in our yard. She had seen me jogging and looked at me with a mixture of wonder and sympathy. In the classroom she acknowledged me with a knowing nod and a half smile. My interview was over. I walked out of the classroom, mulling over whether I'd stretched my "sheep" wide enough.

I did not get in on the day. We were told we had to wait until the end of August when the final admission list would be displayed on the school notice board. If my father was disappointed, he did not show it. He bought me a piece of Bird's Milk cake, which was a treat beyond my dreams. The recipe for the light soufflé on a thin sponge base, covered with glossy dark chocolate, was originally created by the famous Moscow restaurant Praga in 1978. The cake became an instant hit. In the 1980s Soviet citizens from all over the USSR flocked to Praga on a quest for the ultimate delicacy. The queue would disrupt the traffic all the way between Kalinin Street and Arbat. My father explained to me that "bird's milk" was an ancient Greek idiom for something wonderful, unattainable and most desirable.

"Like the sea?" I asked hopefully. I polished off the cake and concocted a new dream. "Like the sea", agreed my father. "As a matter of fact…"

*   *   *

My father, Sergey Bakunin, had followed his parents in choosing a career in academia. As a student who graduated from both school and university with 'red diplomas', a clean slate of top marks, he received an offer to stay at the Physics Faculty of the Ural Polytechnic Institute (now part of the merged UrFU), where he had studied. He got a PhD in analytical chemistry and remained at the faculty until the early 1990s, when changes in the Soviet Union permitted him to try his hand at entrepreneurship. Unlike his father, Sergey never joined the Communist Party and was a bit of a rebel. He and his friends organised Sverdlovsk's first ever discotheque at the Ural Polytechnic Institute, which must have been what clinched him a date with Tatiana, my mother. Be it a dance party or a game of volleyball, a music festival or a May Day demonstration, my father was a master organiser, very happy to be the centre of attention. In August 1986 he was appointed to lead a team of the Institute's students and staff to a sports campus in the Caucasus on the Black Sea, and my mother and I were going with him!

In 1958 the Institute of Agricultural Mechanical Engineering of Rostov-on-Don (now Don State Technical University) began building a recreational sports campus in a place called Divnomorsk (from the Russian for wonderful sea) on the Black Sea, about 300km from Sochi. The campus, called Raduga (rainbow), was built by students and staff on reclaimed land over the course of several summers. In the 1980s Raduga welcomed students and academic staff from universities across the Soviet Union. In June the campus accommodated families with children, while July and August were reserved just for adults who came to stay for three weeks at a time. Full-board accommodation was subsidised by universities and the campus offered basic but comfortable living quarters. It had a very large canteen and two open-air stages for evening entertainment. There were ball courts, an outdoor gym and a large beach. Guests were encouraged to exercise, play games and compete with people from other universities. It was paradise for my father, who loved sports and leading by example.

***

Sitting on a pebble beach and watching other team leaders' children playing in the water was painful. I couldn't swim. My beloved blue ring lay deflated beside me. Earlier when I had dipped my feet in the sea, allowing the water to tickle my toes, my father had called me back: "Either you swim without the ring, or you don't swim at all." My pretence that I was not in the mood for swimming was wearing thin. I walked along the beach, looking for pieces of green bottle glass, smoothed by the sea and buried in the sand. To a preschool girl, this common litter resembled emeralds. I ate some green hazelnuts, crushing their soft shells with pebbles. I went to the sports grounds to see if anyone was playing volleyball or basketball, but games were scheduled for late afternoon, and no one was practising in the heat of the day. I sat in the shade of the Persian silk tree but was tormented by the squeals of joy coming from the water. My father's method of teaching me to swim was harsh but effective. By the end of the afternoon, careful to maintain an expression of being deeply wounded, I stepped into the water. No jellyfish was in sight to give me an excuse to turn back at the last minute. I walked a little further, until the water reached my armpits. *Raz, dva, tri* – on the count of three, I plunged in and started to paddle with the urgency of a dog retrieving a stick. I stopped and then plunged in again, realising that the water was holding me much like my inflatable ring. I could swim.

The next day my father organised a day trip to a remote beach for his team, promising turquoise water and a feast fit for the gods. The food at the canteen followed a recurring theme of boiled sausage with braised cabbage, meatballs with mashed potatoes and buckwheat, flavoured with pork stew. Dessert was often just half a glass of sour cream, which most people used as an after-sun lotion (the real thing was not available in Soviet shops). By contrast, a small daily market nearby was bursting with giant beef tomatoes (called "Ox heart" in Russian), ripe peaches and plums, several varieties of grapes, shameless in their abundance. There were comically shaped peppers untouched by chemical fertilisers, glossy aubergines and pears so fragrant that wasps were cruising over them, seduced by their sweetness. The locals also made traditional Georgian treats called *churchkhella*, a long chewy candy, hanging on a string, made with flour and grape juice and filled with hazelnuts or walnuts. The first stop on our way was this market, where my father put his charm to work to haggle over prices set by the locals. The shops in Divnomorsk, like anywhere else, were bare in comparison to the riches grown in back gardens. It took the best part of an hour to buy enough fruit and vegetables to feed a group of thirty.

My father picked up some pans and cutlery from the canteen, bought whole chickens from a state store, and we marched from Raduga to the beach on the outskirts of Divnomorsk. My father walked first, infecting the rest of the team with his confidence and enthusiasm. He was tall, dressed in white shorts and a white tennis shirt. He looked every inch a leader; a hero from a romantic novel with his dark blonde hair, blue eyes and a trimmed auburn beard. I ran to keep up with his resolute pace.

The beach itself was a picture from an adventure novel, with imposing silver cliffs overlooking the sea, sometimes dropping small pieces of rock on unsuspecting passers-by. The water here was clearer than at the public beach, and some resourceful tourists had discovered a colony of mussels in the shallow sea. My father organised people into teams picking mussels, chopping vegetables for a gigantic dish of ratatouille and gathering wooden debris to make a fire. The mussels were cooked in a pot of sea water. Then everyone joined in, opening shells to pick the soft meat and add it to the vegetables, slowly cooked in an industrial-sized pan. Having never seen fresh seafood before, the tourists sounded like a flock of excited seagulls, tearing warm orange flesh from white stems and sometimes finding tiny pearls inside. Meanwhile, my father grilled chickens on a spit, wearing a makeshift newspaper hat to cover his head from the scorching Caucasus sun. After a day of swimming and sunbathing, mussel picking and cooking, the Sverdlovsk students and academics sat down to enjoy an epicurean feast. In the absence of alcohol (for none was available), imaginary glasses were raised to celebrate my father's ingenuity.

***

In May 1985, almost immediately after coming to power, Mikhail Gorbachev issued a decree aimed at fighting drunkenness and alcoholism in the Soviet Union. The prohibition law, commonly referred to as the 'dry law', restricted sales of alcoholic beverages and raised prices on wine, beer and vodka. Drinking in public places, such as parks and trains, became prohibited. People caught drunk on the street or at work were prosecuted. Most state institutions, including universities, ran government campaigns condemning drinking. Alcohol consumption was banned in Raduga. While it was possible to buy homemade wine and vodka from the locals, students and academic staff caught drinking would be expelled from the campus and risked repercussions at home.

Perhaps inspired by this demand for 'healthier' entertainment, my father organised Raduga's first heptathlon. The events were modified from the Olympic standard and consisted of shooting hoops, a 100m swim, a 5km run, a long jump and a series of timed exercises at the sports grounds, including press-ups, chin-ups and squats. The competition deliberately encompassed multiple disciplines so as not to give an advantage to some accomplished athletes with national championships under their belts. Women as well as men signed up to take part, with less athletic tourists eagerly volunteering to help run the event. My mum made laurels for the winners from vine leaves growing just outside the campus. Some enthusiasts made posters, employing years of experience of making banners for May Day parades. The heptathlon soon became the talk of the town, our own mini-Olympics.

My money was on Valentina, a track athlete from Sverdlovsk. She was not a beauty, as my father remarked. She was scrawny rather than slender and slouched a little. Her drab hair was always tied in a tight ponytail. She wore large glasses with transparent frames, which sat awkwardly on her narrow face. I liked Valentina, because unlike the other female students, who swam with their hair clipped high to protect it from salty water, she swam front crawl all the way to the buoy, without ever stopping for breath. While other girls showed me how to pluck my eyebrows, Valentina taught me how to tie the laces on my trainers so that they stayed put. She did not seem to mind me hanging around her and talking 'race strategy'. Reunited with my blue ring, I set my own record, swimming all the way to the buoy with Valentina, waving to my mum who sat 100m away. Mum suggested Valentina was getting tired of me, but my new friend waved her concerns away and took me to the basketball court to practise shooting hoops, her weakest discipline. I ran after the ricocheted basketball and threw it back, while she cleaned her glasses with a corner of her top in frustration.

On the morning of the heptathlon I raced to the beach before breakfast, briefly forgetting how much I hated running. The sea was thick with hideous jellyfish, but I was not the one about to plunge into the water. Valentina was at the canteen, eating rice porridge she had topped with apricots from the market. She was already wearing running shorts and a stripy red-and-white top with her number clipped to her chest. At a nearby table, competitors from Moscow were laughing and talking over each other. I recognised some of them as star basketball players who had crushed Sverdlovsk men's team in a play-off a week earlier. One man even had a pair of swimming goggles, which looked suspiciously foreign-made. Valentina appeared nonchalant. She offered me an apricot, which must have been expensive. I was too nervous to eat and chewed on a cuticle instead.

Valentina missed quite a few hoops out of her ten attempts, despite my fevered cheering. The beach was just behind the court; she sprinted the distance, dove into the sea, overtook a couple of men on her way and emerged from the water eager to put on her running shoes. Valentina tied the laces twice, just as she had taught me, and ran towards the tarmac road. The road lay between the vineyards and a string of B&Bs and long-term summer rentals along the beach. Instead of following Valentina, I ran to the sports ground near our campus to wait for her there and check out the competition. A hairy-chested man was puffing on the chin-up bar. A ginger beard was counting fifty squats. One of the Muscovites was already on the press-ups, cheered on by a flock of histrionic girls. Valentina appeared suddenly, looking momentarily disoriented without her glasses, then went straight into a long jump. Her dangly legs shot forward, and she landed in the sand a clear leader to a wild whoop from the Sverdlovsk fans. I could not believe that she managed to raise her bony chin to the bar, but she lifted herself, almost gracefully, five times before resting and doing it again. By the time Valentina was on her squats, I had lost my voice. She sprinted for the finish line in front of the open-air stage and raised her lanky arms in the air. When the results had been counted, Valentina, the underdog, had surprised us all – she had come third, defeating the fearsome Muscovites and winning Bronze for Sverdlovsk. In my eyes, she had won Gold.

***

After three weeks on the Russian Riviera, my parents tanned beautifully, while I turned red as a crayfish and peeled. It was time to go home and face the noticeboard of the revered *semidesyatka*. The trouble was that we did not have return tickets. Back in Sverdlovsk, my parents had waited in line for two months, commuting to a travel agency every day after work, taking turns to register their place in a queue for airline tickets. In the end they managed to buy flights to Anapa, a mere three hours by bus from Divnomorsk, but all the flights and trains were full on the way back, with everyone returning home for the start of the school year. From Divnomorsk we were advised to travel to Novorossiysk, a major transport hub on the Black Sea, and try our luck there. At the Novorossiysk railway station my parents left me to guard our luggage, while they stood in different lines, hoping to find seats on a train bound for either Sverdlovsk or Moscow, the central hub of the Soviet rail network. We managed to get on a fast train to Moscow, a twenty-four-hour journey across the Russian steppe.

The open-plan coach was full of holiday-makers on their way home. Inside it smelled of overripe melons, peaches and sticky grapes. We too carried a load of plums, pears and exotic green hazelnuts. The passengers sitting next to us played *Durak* (fool), the most popular Russian card game, idly swatting at pesky flies with folded newspapers. Mum nibbled on roasted sunflower seeds. Father and I killed time with a game of cities, taking it in turns to name Soviet cities beginning with the last letter of the city called by the previous player:

- Leningra*d*!
- *Dushanbe*!
- *Erevan*!
- *Novosibirsk*!
- *Kishinev*!
- *Vilnius*!
- *Sochi*!

I babbled the names as I'd memorised them for the game, never giving a second thought to how these diverse cities of Central Russia and Ukraine, Central Asia and Siberia, the Caucasus and the Carpathians, the Baltic and the Black Sea could ever be united under the political roof of the Soviet Union. Meanwhile, at the other end of the coach someone started playing a guitar and singing the song *Goodbye, America* by a Sverdlovsk rock band Nautilus Pompilius. Its charismatic leader Vyacheslav Butusov started the new wave of music during *perestroika*, which spread from Sverdlovsk to every corner of the country.

> *Goodbye America, oh*
> *The place I've never been to*
> *Goodbye forever*
> *Take a banjo, play for me before I go*

Its bossa nova melody was soon picked up, and the entire coach savoured the sad lyrics, which had become so familiar over the summer nights.

> *Goodbye America, oh*

The place I'll never visit...
Will I hear the song
Which I'll remember forever?

In Moscow Mum bought us roast chicken wrapped in foil from an entrepreneurial babushka who brought her home-cooked food to the railway station and sold it to grateful passengers in transit. Father went to find us seats on one of the Trans-Siberian trains, which went all the way to Vladivostok or Peking and stopped in Sverdlovsk on the way. Hours later, he finally came back with tickets for the train heading to China. He scooped me up along with the luggage and we got into a compartment with Mongolian men occupying two of the four beds and travelling to Ulan-Bator. The last leg of the journey took twenty-five hours of which I mainly remember the outlandish chatter of our fellow passengers, the smell of dried fish and intermittent sleep.

We arrived in Sverdlovsk the evening of the 30th of August. It was already dark but still balmy. My father splashed out on a taxi and loaded me in along with the crate of slightly bruised pears and plums. I fell asleep and could not remember getting home. I was still dreaming of swimming in the sea then swaying in the train when my father woke me up the next day and I found myself in my room with the familiar pale wallpaper and linoleum flooring. For a moment I feared I'd have to go running and clutched my duvet in defence. However, my father was grinning and exclaimed: "Get up, my lord, you have great things to do today!", quoting the French socialist Henri de Saint-Simon. I blinked at him in confusion.

"Tomorrow you are going to school!" he explained triumphantly, picking me up and swirling me around in the air, as if the news wasn't dizzying enough.

Earlier that morning my grandmother had called to report that she'd been to the school the day before to check the final admissions list. My name was on it.

My father was jubilant. Mum regretted me growing up so quickly but had no time to dwell on it: we only had one day to get me ready. She and I raced into town to buy my uniform – a brown dress with a black apron for everyday wear and a white apron for special occasions – white lace to stitch onto the cuffs and the collar of my dress, and ribbons to tie into my hair, which had grown a bit over the summer. My grandparents came over from the other side of Sverdlovsk to give me a shiny rucksack and a bunch of gladioli, explaining that every pupil brought flowers to school on the 1st of September. In one whirlwind of a day, an awkward duckling shed its towelling shorts and turned into a bluestocking with a brand new dress and a pile of scholarly props. In the evening Mum boiled pans of water to scrub me up properly – in those days municipal boiler houses always shut down for the summer.

Chapter III in which little changed but we encountered a pushmi-pullyu

By the end of the 1980s, life in the Soviet Union had changed unrecognisably – for the worse. Ubiquitous shortages gave way to plainly empty shelves. State enterprises began to cut jobs or close down altogether. The government income was insufficient to support the state spending. Schools and hospitals were deprived of funding; pensioners, who had previously enjoyed social security, struggled to make ends meet.

In international waters, the Soviet Union resembled a giant sinking ship. The Berlin Wall fell and pulled down the Soviet influence over Eastern Europe. Even within the Soviet Union, trouble was brewing: in 1988 Armenia and Azerbaijan started a war over the mountainous region Nagorno-Karabakh, locked within Azerbaijan but with an ethnic Armenian majority[2]. In April 1989, Georgian nationalists organised a protest in Tbilisi against Soviet rule. Moscow sent in troops to restore order. In August 1989, on the fiftieth anniversary of the Molotov-Ribbentrop Pact signed between Hitler and Stalin, when Estonia, Latvia and Lithuania had been annexed to the Soviet Union, over two million people in the Baltic

---

2   Nagorno-Karabakh became part of the Soviet Union in the early 1920s as an autonomous region within the Soviet Socialist Republic of Azerbaijan. Following the break-up of the Soviet Union in 1991, Nagorno-Karabakh declared independence, which led to a war in which around 30,000 were killed and more than one million fled their homes. The region's independence has never been recognised. Russia brokered a cease-fire between the Armenians and the Azeri in 1994, but the feud between Armenia and Azerbaijan is ongoing.

republics formed a human chain to call for independence. The USSR was coming apart.

Sverdlovsk, 1989-1991

The swimming pool "Yunost'", with its romantic name meaning "youth", was 50m long. Inside, the Olympic rings and a red flag with Lenin's profile, embossed in gold, hung side by side. Swimming, like every sport in the Soviet Union, was taken very seriously. At the age of nine, I went to "Yunost'" in the mornings before school, training four times a week and every other Saturday. My teacher, Olga Vladimirovna, was a former national champion. She was less cruel than my gymnastics teachers, who intimidated me for two years then culled me from the club for weighing 21kg at the age of six. Olga Vladimirovna was also less snobbish than my ballroom dancing teachers, who trialled me for a couple of months then dismissed me for lack of musicality. I was awkward at figure skating and not tall enough for volleyball; I was too slow for athletics but I was not altogether hopeless at swimming. I was praised for good technique, especially my backstroke, even if I never won any competitions. Born at the end of December, I was small for my year group. If not for the overwhelming stench of chlorine, the greenish shimmer my blonde hair acquired, the scaly skin on my arms and legs, I could have enjoyed swimming...

After a morning teaching breaststroke and front crawl, Olga Vladimirovna dismissed the class with a loud whistle, which probably startled even the speed skaters at the stadium outside. I hurried to the changing room, looking forward to the reliably scrumptious lunch that awaited me at the house of my maternal grandmother, Baba Tonya or Babushka, as I called her. The popular school No. 70 was so full that second and third formers had their classes in the afternoon from two o'clock. Babushka lived only five minutes' walk from the swimming pool, but I was not about to get frostbite at -25°C. I put on my brown cotton tights, followed by black wool pants, a scratchy wool dress and a heavy jumper. I wore thick socks my babushka had knitted for me, and black *valenki*, soft felt boots. I coiled a scarf twice around my neck, put on a rabbit fur hat and my faux fur coat, spotted like a leopard. I pushed open the heavily frosted door and ventured outside.

It was snowing. Soft flakes danced down slowly, covering the hardened layer of snow on the pavements like cotton wool. The fresh snow crunched gently under my *valenki*, creating a sense of fairy-tale magic in the middle of the busy city. I was lost in a daydream when I remembered a treat lying in my pocket. I took off my mittens and found a small square of bubble gum, wrapped in colourful imported paper. It said "Donald Duck", and indeed Disney's character smiled at me conspiratorially. Quickly, before I lost feeling in my fingers, I unwrapped the gum. Inside there was an insert with a cartoon featuring Donald and his friend Goofy. It was a new insert to add to my precious collection. The gum was white and rock solid. I popped it into my mouth, careful not to lick my lips so they didn't crack later. The gum crumbled like shortbread after its exposure to the Russian frost. Still, it was sweet and tasted thrillingly foreign. By the time I got to my grandmother's flat, I was covered in snow from head to toe, my nose and cheeks glowing like a robin's chest. When my grandmother opened the door, I blew a bubble and popped it.

***

Antonina (Tonya) Berseneva, my maternal grandmother, was born in 1914 in a small town called Revda, 50km from Sverdlovsk. Revda is one of the oldest towns in the Urals. It was founded back in 1734, when Demidovs, the famous industrial dynasty, built an ironworks plant there. Today the town is home to some of the largest mining, metallurgical and construction companies in the region. Tonya studied bookkeeping and worked as a chief accountant at a construction factory in Revda, where Boris Yeltsin, Russia's first president, had worked as a managing director before he turned to politics. Babushka spoke little of her earlier life. In fact, I only recall one curious story about a goat. My grandmother's family kept a goat, which produced plenty of milk, but in the time of Bolshevik push for industrialisation and *raskulachivaniye* (stripping land and livestock off wealthy peasants), the animal caused embarrassment to Tonya, the schoolgirl. She told me she had used to hide when her teachers came to the house to buy goat's milk. Babushka didn't talk about her career either, but in my first couple of years at school, she often checked my maths homework, making calculations on a wooden abacus or in her head. She got married to Peter Bersenev, and they had three children, Rudolph, Ludmila and my mother Tatiana, their youngest. Sadly, Peter (Deda Petya) died from a heart attack when I was still a toddler. Babushka lived on her own for a further twenty years, spending a fair amount of time looking after her three grandchildren and two great-grandchildren.

***

"Will you come to the shop with me?" my grandmother asked.

Babushka was almost seventy-five and now relied on a walking stick for longer outings. I knew she was not fond of it though, and preferred holding my arm for support. I dropped my swimming bag and helped my babushka put on her well-worn black faux fur coat. Just around the corner from her block of flats there was a small store with a grand sign, "Fruit and Vegetables", in oversized maroon letters. Inside, dried-up carrots, sprouting potatoes and beetroot caked in mud all made for a sorry sight. There was a mound of rotting onions and little else on the 'state' side of the store. A bored vendor sat at the till wearing an old-fashioned starched white cap on top of her bleached hair, which was tied in a loose bun. Next to her, in the corner of the store, was a 'co-operative' section. There a selection of fruit with foreign stickers was sold at higher prices, reflecting the real value of oranges, apples and grapes. Babushka made a mental calculation and whispered to me that a kilo of 'state' onions cost the same as a single 'co-operative' grape. I nodded, spotting a small pile of grape seeds lying at the till next to the vendor. Oblivious to my accusing stare, the vendor continued inspecting her nails. Baba Tonya sighed and we left the store.

The street was empty; only a few cars passed by, their wipers working overtime to clear the front windows from falling snow. Baba Tonya and I walked slowly, wary of the icy patches on the road, invisible under the fluffy carpet. We crossed the road and walked towards a large universal store opposite the botanical gardens that Babushka was so fond of visiting during the summer months. Just a few years earlier, the universal store had been considered one of the best in Sverdlovsk, with a reliable supply of staple groceries and even occasional treats like fresh herring, crab butter and imported olives. By 1989, things had changed dramatically. Every day people formed a long queue, weaving through the specially erected metal barriers that regulated the crowd. They hoped to find basic food like bread, grains and dairy, and to buy meat or ham using ration coupons. As we approached the store, Baba Tonya gripped her bag tighter, worried someone would try to grab it and run away. She'd seen that happen before. We joined the queue. The snow kept falling, pretty and gentle, but it gave little solace to the hungry, dispirited people, no longer singing *chastushki* about Gorbachev but angry about their new circumstances.

This store too was nearly empty, save for the cooperative section. Strange things were on display there: imported margarine, which apparently required no refrigeration, and vacuum-packed salami and cheese, already sliced! People gathered around the display, studying it like a precious artefact in a museum. Someone lifted a yellow tub of margarine and tried to sniff it through the plastic. A man wearing an *ushanka,* a fur hat with ear flaps, lifted a piece of salami with unveiled disgust and said to no one in particular: "So this is what Gorbachev is eating now!" Realising there was no one with whom to pick a fight and vent his anger, the man dropped his impromptu weapon, surrendering to misery. Babushka sighed even deeper this time. She bought a piece of boiled *kolbasa* (ham) with her monthly coupon, no doubt for my benefit. At home she made a simple potato soup, which she knew was my favourite. She opened the fridge to find her last piece of butter and added it to the potatoes. She cut a slice of *kolbasa*, slowly diced it into smaller pieces and carefully put them into a pan. The smell of fried meat was some comfort.

Babushka's kitchen was tiny but light. Three people would be a crowd inside it. Baba Tonya's children and grandchildren relied on her always having something on the stove or in the oven. My mother had a particular weakness for her fish pie with pastry that Babushka naturally made herself from scratch. There was always a clay pot, dusted in flour, covered with a cloth that Babushka had embroidered with a pattern of rowanberry, which stood on top of a radiator, the heat helping the dough to rise. My cousin Anton loved *zrazy*, potato cakes, filled with mincemeat, dusted in cornmeal and pan-fried. My uncle Rudolph was partial to *seledka pod shuboy*, "herring under a fur coat", a traditional Russian dish in which the herring was lavishly covered with a ruby coat of cooked potatoes, carrots, beetroot, onions and dill, dressed with mayonnaise. Perhaps, having lived through the Revolution, the famine of the 1930s and the Great Patriotic War, Baba Tonya could not help but want to feed her family, always cooking a large pot and insisting on us having seconds (not that anyone ever refused). Like my other grandparents, she too ate each meal with a piece of bread. After we finished the soup topped with fried ham, Babushka took out her needles and started knitting, her fingers moving in time with the tick tock of a cuckoo clock on the wall. Everything in the kitchen – the aloe plant on a window sill, enamel pots on the stove, a cupboard where Babushka kept her flour, sugar and lentils supplied by the State in an effort to support the pensioners, a fridge filled with homemade pickles and jams, simple stools and squeaky floorboards – all seemed frozen in time, preserved as a still-life testament to a world held dear but increasingly outdated. An old samovar was still the centrepiece of the table, but its shine was now dull from cooking fumes. It reflected a selection of Donald Duck inserts I had collected from bubble gum packets and had lovingly laid down on the table after lunch. Unlike a treasure preserved from the past, this new bounty appeared to have been brought back from the future.

***

I discovered bubble gum through my school friend Anya. Anya's father was an engineer sent by the Soviet Union to assist our Communist brothers in Yemen. Her family had lived there for two years before returning to Sverdlovsk in time for her to start school. Anya was worldly. She had a cassette stereo player at home and a poster of Vyacheslav Butusov from Nautilus Pompilius on her wall. She had a pair of jeans! Sometimes she even ate lunch at a public canteen rather than at home if her mother, who worked in the Department of Pensions, did not have time to cook and gave her pocket money instead. It was an awfully grown up thing to do at the age of nine. Most of the time Anya just bought a *bublik*, a poppy seed bagel, at the bakery and spent the rest of the money on bubble gum and imported chocolate.

Her collection of Donald Duck inserts was unrivalled until another classmate of ours, deemed unpopular for wearing glasses, turned up to school with a whole stash of imported goodies her mother had brought back from a business trip to Helsinki. Anya and I were green with envy. We had to act.

Anya came up with a plan. She nicked a few cigarettes from her mother's bag to sell to older children in her neighbourhood. By the third form we could produce a convincing British accent and read such simple labels as "king size" embossed in tiny golden letters on each cigarette. We thought the reference to royalty would be our trump card, but the older boys smelled our desperation and gave us one rouble for the entire booty. Still, a rouble was enough to buy a strip of Donald Duck chewing gum from the private vendors at *avtovokzal*, a nearby intercity bus station.

With *perestroika*, small trade changed *avtovokzal* from a boring station to a busy commercial junction. Just as a toy bus dropped into the sea is soon enveloped by weed, so was *avtovokzal's* primary function transformed into the centre of *chelnok* trade. *Chelnok* was a small businessman or woman who travelled to Turkey (which allowed short stays without visas for Russians), bought cheap clothes, shoes and sweets at the Istanbul bazaars and carried the bulky sacks back to Russia to make a small profit. Sweets were sold in small kiosks (or *palatki* as they are called in Moscow), which had popped up like mushrooms after the rain on every Russian street corner. Counterfeit Adidas shoes, Dolce & Gabbana t-shirts and other apparel were sold in markets that opened daily near *avtovokzaly* all over Russia. The word "shopping" entered Russian vocabulary and became a popular hobby.

Avtovokzal was also the playground for private vendors offering 'better' deals to gullible shoppers. Anya and I approached a fidgety fellow who held a bright strip of gum in the air as bait. He grabbed our rouble all too quickly and disappeared. The plastic wrap around the strip of gums turned out to be folded rather than sealed. Unwrapping one of the gums revealed no liner inside. Instead of bubble gum, we found plasticine.

***

My first year at school No. 70 was a timid affair. On the very first day of school, nervous first formers lined up at a festive assembly in the school's gymnasium. I was the third pupil from the 'tail', ranked by my height. Still holding flowers we had all brought in for the occasion, we sang the national anthem, then followed our teachers upstairs into the classrooms, leaving emotional parents behind. Together with forty other pupils, I was put into class B, with B standing for less able than A, although not as hopeless as C – arbitrary labels, which while undeserved and secret, were effective in establishing class rivalry. Our teacher, Zoya Aleksandrovna, with her bulging eyes and a prominent mole at the base of her nose, was fond of reminding us that we were nothing but a herd of rams. Rams (*barany* in Russian) were stupid, undisciplined and abbreviated in Zoya Aleksandrovna's mind to the letter B. (Interestingly, C students were told that B stood for *blat* (an informal word for achievement through connections and contacts, rather than on merit or via official means.) I was among the slowest readers. My handwriting was slanted too far left against the standard Russian right incline. I showed some promise at drawing but no aptitude for music. The highlight of that first year was playing "tsar of the mountain" on a snow pile after school. Perhaps the war theme of the schoolyard game was inspired by the gas mask-fitting practice we all had to do in case the Soviet Union came under nuclear attack. Fighting for my place at the top of the pile, I shoved my classmate Alesha Vesely away so fiercely that he fell head down and hit the ice rink. Relieved he had not died, Anya and I went to her nearby flat, where her mother treated us to an orange (a rare treat) while Alesha was receiving stitches to his head.

My father was not too pleased when I received fives and fours (As and Bs) at the end of my first academic year, promptly reminding me that he had always been a straight five student.

"Do you know that your classmate Ksenia Zvyagina sat at the back of the classroom during the parents' meeting and read *The Master and Margarita*? Now, that's a bright girl," he once told me meaningfully.

It took me a couple of years, but eventually I pulled up and got five in every quarter of every year in every subject. (It took me a bit longer to become friends with Ksenia.) The Soviet school system did not rely on end-of-year exams or big tests to grade pupils; rather, our homework was constantly marked, and we were awarded grades for proving a geometry theorem on a blackboard, telling the class about the battle of Borodino in a history lesson or reciting irregular English verbs. Alongside literature classes, we studied Russian. It took eight years of school to master the spelling, grammar and punctuation of our magnificent language. Russian, mathematics and English were the most emphasised subjects on the school curriculum. "Excellent" academically, I was also a troublemaker, my school records stained by "satisfactory" and "unsatisfactory" marks for behaviour.

One particularly crimson episode involved beetroot. During home economy classes, girls were taught to sew, embroider and cook, while boys built stools and learned how to fix a short circuit. When we swapped for a few lessons, girls also had a basic electronics class and boys learned how to sew an apron and cook potatoes. It was during the first culinary class that girls were split into several groups to cook a classic Russian salad, *vinegret*. It is a simple salad of diced cooked beetroot, carrots, potatoes, tinned green peas, sauerkraut and pickled cucumbers dressed with oil or mayonnaise. Each of us had to bring boiled vegetables so that we could dice them during class and assemble the dish. Mum boiled me a beetroot the size of a large grapefruit. I had just managed to peel it when Irina Vasil'yevna, an immaculately tidy teacher with thin lips, a golden tooth and a high coiffure, asked me to recite the rules of how to use a knife. It was our homework. It was one of many occasions when my tactical approach to homework ("Surely she won't actually ask us in class?") backfired. Irina Vasil'yevna quickly grasped that I hadn't a clue and asked me to *read* the rules instead. I reached for the brand new textbook, completely forgetting to wipe my beetroot-stained fingers first. I was made to stay after class and wash the floor, whilst Irina Vasil'yevna made a note in my academic diary: "Bakunina ruined a textbook with beetroot." She also observed that with my floor washing skills, leaving gaps between the strokes, I would get a gap-toothed husband.

After the first three years of elementary school, Zoya Aleksandrovna shed crocodile tears and passed us on to a host of new teachers, each eager to remind us that their subject should take priority. In Russia we revered our teachers (even if we didn't like them), but no one inspired as much awe as Alevtina Aleksandrovna, who taught algebra and geometry. Her posture was as straight as her ruler, and she usually wore a pleated skirt, a light blouse and a jacket, never a casual jumper or a cardigan. She commanded absolute authority and was strict, but fair.

Alevtina Aleksandrovna and I got off on the wrong foot. One day just after the beginning of the second term of my fourth year, she asked my mother to come and see her. My mother had assumed it was to do with the homework I had not done when there had been a power cut, and we had been short on candles. Alevtina Aleksandrovna received my mother with courtesy but got straight down to business.

"Yana was reading a book during my mathematics class. It was *fiction*."

Grave silence set in. Outside the schoolyard was dark, the only light coming from the windows of the block of flats opposite the school building. My mother was clearly in shock because she finally asked:

"What was the book?"

"*Tomek's Adventures in Gran Chaco*," replied Alevtina Aleksandrovna and raised one eyebrow.

Mother nodded. She wished her husband was with her, or her parents-in-law, well-spoken, charismatic academics who could plead my case.

She looked at the teacher and said: "Alevtina Aleksandrovna, Yana is a good girl, a bright girl; she does her homework, she reads, she loves a challenge, perhaps if you were to show her some attention... Look here, she got fives in every subject other than maths last quarter..."

Alevtina Aleksandrovna looked at my mother, who was clearly nervous, her eyes now glistening behind her glasses, her voice steady but not without effort. This mother *cared*.

"Did she?" said the teacher, narrowing her eyes and pressing her lips simultaneously, as was her habit. "I'll see what I can do."

The very next day Alevtina Aleksandrovna asked me to solve a problem at the blackboard in front of the class. Unaware of the previous evening's conference, I took a piece of chalk and solved the problem with confidence. I got a five. Alevtina Aleksandrovna started testing me often, marking my homework, asking me to speak up during her classes, just when I least expected it. She truly was on my case. Whether I wanted that kind of attention or not, I took it in my stride. At the end of that quarter just before the New Year break, I got my five in maths. I became an all-round five student and I kept that unblemished record until graduation day. Alevtina Aleksandrovna remained relentlessly strict with us until the very last lesson, but somehow even pupils who hated maths, never spoke of her with anything but respect.

In the fourth grade we also started learning history, which was taught by Galina Il'inichna, a name even Russians would break their tongues to pronounce, so we called her Galinishna instead. Galinishna was also responsible for looking after the welfare of senior pupils, a role she had been born for.

She looked like a larger-than-life mother hen protective of her chicks, regardless of the trouble they'd caused. Anya and I had once tried to teach English to Iraida Leonidovna, an old cleaning lady who had been so intimidated by us that she complained to Galinishna about being harassed. By that point Anya and I had been up to so much mischief we feared expulsion. Galinishna called us into her office, looking every inch Lady Justice with her henna-dyed hair tied back in the Greek style and wearing a loosely fitting robe. Towering over her desk, she went through all our shenanigans, then assumed a dispassionate expression to listen to our profuse apologies. I tried to conjure a mental picture of my father finding out about my expulsion, but my imagination failed me. Anya, who later made a career in PR, shuffled forward and said: "Galinina Il'inichna, what can we do to redeem our appalling behaviour?"

"I might have an idea, yes," said Galinishna, smiling, "Since you two appear to be so creatively talented, I'd like you to help me organise a school celebration of the Olympic Games in the assembly hall. As you know, 1988 was a unique year during which both the Winter Olympics took place in Calgary and the Summer Olympics in Seoul. Write me a script, recruit others to help you and we'll produce a stage show, celebrating the history of the Olympic Games from the days of Ancient Greece until today. Obviously, you'll have to do all the work after school on top of your regular homework..."

We put on a cracking show, with narrators dressed in bed sheets-cum-togas giving a live history lesson of the Olympic glory. The culmination of the show was Moscow 1980. We dressed our tallest classmate in Anya's father's bear fur coat, and he produced a decent Russian folk dance on stage, despite dripping with sweat. Even Iraida Leonidovna, the cleaning lady, clapped in delight. Wise Galinishna was also *the* go-to person for career advice. My classmate Kseniya Zvyagina told her she hoped to become an archaeologist. Galinishna put her motherly arm over Kseniya's shoulders and said: "Dear child, if you became an archaeologist, you'd spend six months in a tent in a remote steppe. How would you hope to start a family?" Needless to say, Kseniya decided against the spinster route and became an HR director instead.

***

It was Galinishna who helped us understand why Russia has been forever torn by invisible forces, pulling it in opposite directions by the conflicting ideologies of the East and the West. The country's geography, spanning both Asia and Europe, gives the first visual clue, but it's the history that reveals the deeply ingrained origins of the often misunderstood Russian psyche and cultural heritage.

Russia's early history stems from the middle of the ninth century when Varangian chieftain Ryurik built a settlement near Novgorod (in the European part of modern Russia) for his tribe, Rus'. Varangians were migrants from Scandinavia who had crossed the Baltic Sea and landed in Eastern Europe. Ryurik was the first chieftain to unite and settle nomadic Eastern Slavs. His successor Oleg travelled down the river Dnieper to a town called Kiev (today's capital of Ukraine), strategically well positioned on the trading route between

Scandinavia and Constantinople. Oleg took Kiev in 882 and formed a new state: Kievan Rus'.

Oleg's great-grandson Vladimir decided to establish a state religion. He had considered a number of available faiths and settled upon Greek Orthodoxy, thereby allying Kievan Rus' with Constantinople and the West. (Allegedly he decided against Islam because he believed that his people could not live under a religion that prohibited alcohol.) Kievan Rus' was christened in 988, which led to the Slavs being introduced to Greek philosophy, history and science.

In the thirteenth century, following an internal power struggle between the heirs to the throne, Rus' gradually disintegrated into regional fragments and was invaded by Tatar-Mongols, led by the grandson of Genghis-Khan. The Tatar-Mongols destroyed most of the cities (Kiev and Vladimir never recovered their status after the devastation) and established an exorbitant tax system, under which regional princes made regular contributions to the Tatar-Mongol Empire of the Golden Horde. The economic development of Rus' stalled, the country lost a third of its population to violence and mass murders, and its culture became 'confused' by the Asian and nomadic influence of its conquerors. At the same time, that 'dark' period of Tatar-Mongol oppression helped to unite the fragmented territory. In 1380 a regional prince Dmitriy Donskoy, based in a town called Moskva (Moscow) on the confluence of the Moskva and Neglina rivers, attacked and defeated the Golden Horde army in battle at Kulikovo. The Tatar-Mongols retaliated and dominated Russia for another century. Finally, in 1480 Ivan the Great fought them off, and his son Ivan IV (Ivan the Terrible) finished the job in 1552.

He built St. Basil's Cathedral in Moscow to commemorate his victory and united Russia under the new capital city.

The Romanov dynasty came to power in 1613. The most prominent of the Romanovs, Peter I (also known as Peter the Great), started his reign at the end of the seventeenth century with a tour of Europe, which inspired him to modernise Russia and westernise its society. When Peter returned to Russia, he ordered a fleet to be built, introduced military conscription, re-wrote laws and changed the way the nobles dressed. He was a hands-on ruler, personally clipping the beards of the Russian nobility. With his new fleet, Peter sought to improve Russia's access to the ocean. The Black Sea was at the time controlled by the Ottoman Empire. Peter made an agreement with Poland, which ceded Kiev back to Russia and waged war against the Tatars in the Crimea, controlled by the Ottoman sultan. By the end of the seventeenth century, Peter defeated the Crimean khan and established Russia's first naval base in Taganrog on the Azov Sea, giving it access to the Black Sea. Peter also fought the Swedes to acquire access to the Baltic Sea, gaining control over Ukraine, Latvia, Estonia and parts of Finland. In 1703 he founded Saint Petersburg on the Gulf of Finland, transferring the capital of Russia from Moscow to the brand new city.

The future direction of Russia was hotly debated in the middle of the nineteenth century during the reign of Nikolai I. Two schools of thought emerged, calling themselves "Westerners" and "Slavophiles". Inspired by Peter the Great, the Westerners called for the modernisation of Russia, the abolition of serfdom, the adoption of European practices. The Slavophiles scorned the West and advocated

"Orthodoxy, Autocracy and National Spirit". The National Spirit emphasised national identity, the integrity of Russia and implied unity between ruler and people. The Slavophiles cursed Peter the Great for "hacking the window into Europe" and sidestepping Russia's "unique divine path". Nikolai I was all for the National Spirit. The Crimean war at the end of his reign revealed the political vulnerabilities and the economic backwardness of Russia.

Alexander II finally abolished serfdom in 1861, reformed the privileges of the nobility and reorganised the judicial system, but his reforms were not considered progressive enough. Proponents of a constitutional monarchy, socialists and anarchists were all plotting against the government. These plotters included Mikhail Bakunin, the father of Russia's anarchist movement, who fought over ideology with Karl Marx. Alexander II planned to announce an elected parliament, *Duma*, but he held back and was assassinated in 1881, which effectively ended any possibility of Russia becoming a constitutional monarchy.

The last Russian tsar, Nikolai II, acceded to the throne in 1894. The Japanese attacked Russia's eastern border in January 1905. At the same time, there was mass political and social unrest, including strikes by the workers, riots among the peasants and military mutiny, which spread throughout the empire, culminating in a workers' procession to the Winter Palace in Saint Petersburg to deliver a petition to the tsar. Government troops opened fire, killing many demonstrators. This gave rise to Russia's first revolution. As a result, Nikolai II was forced to establish the Duma but he too failed to implement reforms bold enough to address the rapidly changing shape of Russian society – industrialisation and the development of oil fields in Baku had created a large social class of dissident workers. To compound the problem, Russia's involvement in the First World War had devastating consequences for the economy and destroyed morale. The revolution of 1917 was, in short, inevitable.

By February 1917 riots and mutiny were widespread. The Duma approved the establishment of the so-called Provisional Government to restore order. Nikolai II abdicated the throne. While the Provisional Government, first with a liberal democrat, then with a socialist at its helm, tried to make sense of the chaos engulfing the country, Bolsheviks (members of the majority), the larger left-wing faction of the Russian Socialist Democratic Labour Party, gained overwhelming popularity among workers' *soviets* (councils). In October 1917, the Bolsheviks, led by Vladimir Lenin, overthrew the Provisional Government and seized control of Russia. The Civil War followed. The "Reds" (the Bolsheviks) defeated the "Whites" (everyone else who disagreed with their Communist ideology). The Union of Soviet Socialist Republics was formed in 1922. By 1940, the Soviet Union had grown from the four founding republics (Russia, Ukraine, Belorussia and the Caucasus) to sixteen, covering one sixth of the total landmass of the world.

***

Galinishna was fanning herself with a yellow exercise book, her gaze following wisps of poplar fluff waltzing in the air outside. Without turning around, she announced that we had ten minutes to finish the history test. It was May 1991 and the final week of the fifth form. Despite the windows being open, the classroom was hot. The sparrows were chirping noisily, making it maddeningly difficult to concentrate on the test. A droplet of sweat trickled down the neck of Sasha Starkov sitting in front of me. The navy jacket of his school uniform was buttoned up, his breathing laborious. Next to me Natasha Radchenko was red either from the heat or from the shame of having forgotten to wear her pioneer neckerchief to school. Without it, her brown uniform looked bland, like the food served at the school canteen. Across the aisle Irina Lunina was writing with her mouth open, her tongue sticking out comically. I re-read the last paragraph of the essay I'd written, briefly distracted by the purple ink blots on my white cuffs. My sleeves also seemed too short all of a sudden, as I had sprung up in height. My essay was good though, I was sure of it. I had chosen to write about the ideological debate between the Westerners and the Slavophiles, comparing Russia to the fictional pushmi-pullyu[3] (a Hugh Lofting character from Doctor Doolittle children's books), with its two heads pulling and pushing Russia in opposite directions forever after.

I put the pen down and looked outside. A five in history was in the bag, as was my clean slate of fives in all other subjects for the year. I could not wait for the summer holidays: a month at a pioneer camp, subsidised by my grandfather's university, a month at the *dacha* and then a vacation with my parents. There was my grandmother's birthday to look forward to, with the usual feast of home-cooked delicacies: shortages or not, a family gathering was unthinkable without

---

3   *Tyani-tolkay* in Russian

bliny with caviar, cured ham, homemade pickles and pies, *vinegret*, *seledka pod shuboy*, *kholodets* (braised beef in jelly), mum's favourite fish pie, and a birthday cake, its icing made with imported margarine in the absence of butter.

Chapter IV in which I got a taste of zagranitsa

By 1991 most of the Soviet republics made it clear that they wanted greater independence from Moscow. Gorbachev reacted by drafting a "New Union Treaty" which was to decentralise much of the power and make the Soviet Union a federation of independent republics. Some thought that the new treaty was not radical enough, while a few old Party cadres felt quite the opposite. Eight communist hardliners, including the head of the KGB, organised a coup d'état.

They detained Gorbachev under house arrest at his *dacha* in the Crimea, took over the state media and mobilised the army. On August 19th 1991 the Emergency Committee, as they called themselves, announced their plans to restore the "honour and dignity" of the Soviet Union. Unfortunately for them, the President of the Russian Republic, Boris Yeltsin, put together a rapid counterattack, calling on citizens to stand up against the reactionary coup. His cause was helped significantly by the main national television channel covering the events and juxtaposing old, orthodox Emergency Committee members with the energetic, passionate Russian president. On August 20th 1991 the Emergency Committee attacked the White House, Russia's government building, but its defenders were prepared and the coup was over by the next day. The instigators were arrested. Gorbachev returned to Moscow but the balance of power had tipped towards Yeltsin.

The unsuccessful coup changed everything. By the end of 1991, the Soviet Union was dissolved.

My father was not one of those people cursing the television screen at the start of *The Projector of Perestroika*, a popular daily programme reporting on the progress (what else?) of restructuring. Nor was he trembling at the prospect of being laid off or mourning the stability of the previous decades. Only Party *nomenklatura*, members of the KGB or people with connections and therefore jobs *"po blatu"* (rather than through merit), lived well in the Soviet days. A modest research fellow and lecturer at a polytechnic, Sergey Bakunin saw *perestroika* as an opportunity to better his life.

My father was thirty-five when he met representatives of an East German optics manufacturer, Karl Zeiss, at a scientific conference in Moscow. A year later in 1990, initially with the support of his institute, he opened a showroom at his faculty, which was equipped with the latest microscopes and other analytical devices delivered by Karl Zeiss and financed by two major Sverdlovsk industrial companies. Both academics and industrial specialists had access to his state-of-the-art lab. Just when my father had persuaded some of the major manufacturing enterprises in the Urals to trial Karl Zeiss equipment, the government announced that it would be closing down the fixed exchange rate scheme for state-owned enterprises. Anticipating exposure to the actual exchange rates for foreign currencies, the local manufacturers rushed to order machinery from my father's newly incorporated company. Before he could walk as an entrepreneur, Sergey Bakunin left the Ural Polytechnic Institute to run his own business importing industrial and consumer goods from Germany. His firm bought and sold eyewear, used cars, foods and apparel, tableware and furniture. It was an entirely opportunistic venture with its triumphs and disasters, the latter caused mostly by the rigid bureaucracy and backwardness of the Russian trade customs and commercial laws.

My father's work took him on many business trips to Germany. Every time he came back with plenty of presents for my mother and me. He loved bringing home foreign treats to surprise us with. Once my father arrived late at night, but of course he woke us up, spreading out his bounty on the table. I remember the rest of the tower blocks around us covered in darkness. There was something mischievous about feasting on foreign fruit when everyone else was asleep. That night we ate kiwi fruit for the first time. We had no idea it was supposed to be peeled. We washed and ate it skin and all, labelling the exotic fruit as a giant sweeter version of a Russian gooseberry. Another time he brought home a pineapple. I had never seen a pineapple before, other than in an illustration from a Soviet classic, *A Book of Tasty and Healthy Food* (which featured many exotic ingredients such as scallops and capers, which were unimaginable in Soviet shops, yet created an illusion of plenty). Needless to say, we never dared to cut the pineapple and it eventually rotted on its pedestal in our living room. Thanks to my father's gifts, my picture of *zagranitsa* (abroad) filled up like a colouring book from subtle contours to a kaleidoscope of chocolate, exotic fruit, eye-catching clothes, shiny stationery and alien home appliances. (Whoever had heard of a cordless phone or an electric meat grinder?) In contrast to everything made in the Soviet Union, most foreign goods were flamboyantly bright.

My first pair of jeans were green as an autumn leaf about to turn yellow. Father must have bought them on sale for the colour was not conventionally attractive, but for a ten-year-old Soviet schoolgirl it didn't matter. I packed my jeans to change into after *fizkultura* (physical education) at the end of the school day. I was desperate to be noticed by my classmates, but the only comment I got was from Irina Lunina, who walked with me to the tram stop and said: "Bakunina, what are *those*?" "Why, jeans, of course!" I replied, beaming. "Those aren't jeans, Bakunina, jeans are blue. And *that* – I don't know what colour it is – but it's not blue." With that Lunina hopped on a tram and was off before I could argue back. I got on a different tram to visit Baba Tonya, where instead of moral support I got "girls ought to wear skirts not trousers".

My first pocket calculator was another false friend. It was the size of my palm and just a couple of millimetres thin. It was handy for algebra classes, and I hid it under my exercise books. When, during an algebra test, Alevtina Aleksandrovna spotted me pressing the tiny buttons, her face turned white as chalk then purple. She confiscated the device and gave me a *kol* (the lowest possible mark, only attainable through gross misconduct), shaming me in front of the entire class. It took months to earn enough top marks to bring my average grade to "excellent" and win back the revered teacher's goodwill. I used my calculator at home but I dared not bring it to school. Later in life I thought of Alevtina Aleksandrovna and her professional ethics with gratitude for my numeracy.

The most precious present I received from my father was a walkman. I was about eleven, and my walkman was the envy of the entire school. Older school children, who never ordinarily mingled with juniors, stopped me in corridors and asked to look at my gadget. It did not matter that at the time I only had two tapes to play. One was an album by a West-German R&B and pop band, Milli Vanilli, which was quite possibly the first ever sound of rap heard in Ekaterinburg. The second cassette was a recordable one. A few of my friends had stereos at home. They would spend hours in the evening listening to the radio and recording songs onto tapes. It took skill and patience but in the absence of official albums, every creaky recording of Roxette or Brian Adams was priceless. We'd listen to music on my walkman during school breaks and even deliberately be a minute late to class just to say "We missed the bell because we were listening to music on a *walkman*" to annoy the physics teacher whom we neither liked nor feared.

Our family could now afford "co-operative" and imported foods. For breakfast, instead of *tvorog*, the traditional cottage cheese, with sour cream and home-made jam, I preferred *yogurt* and *müsli*. It was strange to eat raw oat flakes but I adored sweet yogurt in various flavours, completely oblivious to its sugar content and other ingredients, which gave it its long life, necessary to survive the Soviet and then Russian customs. On Monday 19th August 1991, we sat down for breakfast in the living room, and my father turned on the TV, as was his habit. He liked watching the news at the beginning and end of each day. That morning instead of the usual programme there was a broadcast of a special announcement, "The Appeal to the Soviet People", read out in a deep, grave voice. The address explained that due to Mikhail Gorbachev's "ill health", the newly formed Emergency Committee was to assume power in order to restore order after years of chaos and the "age-old friendship in the unified family of fraternal people and the revival of the fatherland". We sat at the table, too stunned to speak. Eventually, my mum, who sat facing the screen, rather than the table, turned back and looked at my father in shock.

"What does it mean?" she said, not disguising her fear.

"I don't know", which was unthinkable, coming from my father.

Listening to the broadcast, I could not pretend to understand its content, but the solemn tone of the speaker was so radically different from the usual upbeat programmes of the *perestroika* era that the news appeared undoubtedly grim. The man kept repeating the words *rodina* (motherland) and *otechestvo* (fatherland) as if the country was in danger, but it was not clear who or what was the threat. At the end of the announcement, our living room filled with the sound of mournful classical music. For the next few hours the TV channels played recordings of the Bolshoi's Swan Lake and repeated the Emergency Committee's address. My father explained to me that traditionally during dramatic events, such as the death of a leading official, classical music and ballet replaced the regular TV programming. My parents feared that Gorbachev was dead.

Later in the day the Emergency Committee gave a press conference which was broadcast live. The central figure on our screen was Gennadiy Yanaev, formerly an unimportant cog in Gorbachev's government. He was joined by other members of the Emergency Committee, all of them old party hardliners. Yanaev sat hunched over a desk, his suit creased at the top of the shoulders. His hands trembled.

"Trembling hands are a sign of a chicken thief", said mum, reciting an old Russian saying.

That night we were back at the table, once again glued to the screen. The evening news programme, *Vremya* (Time), began with the stony-faced announcers quoting the "Appeal to the Soviet People" and warning viewers of the impending chaos and lawlessness. Quite unexpectedly, *Vremya* switched to a live broadcast from the centre of Moscow. We saw tanks rolling onto the Red Square past the famous St. Basil's Cathedral. The trolleybuses were positioned to block the traffic, providing a corridor for the tanks. We saw confused-looking soldiers and anxious civilians pouring onto the streets. We saw people reading leaflets and eventually the cameras zoomed in on a man standing on top of a tank, his towering figure dominating the screen. At once we recognised our *zemlyak* (a local), Boris Yeltsin.

Yeltsin was born and brought up in the Urals. In 1985, he was ignited by Gorbachev's ideas of *perestroika* and offered him full support. A member of the Communist Party in Sverdlovsk, Yeltsin was invited to come to Moscow and soon became a member of the governing Central Committee of the Communist Party of the Soviet Union. However, by 1987 Yeltsin became disillusioned. He resigned from the Committee, citing a massive gap between Gorbachev's ideas in principle and the actual reforms as well as the dysfunctional Committee, whose dinosaur members were deliberately stalling the new policies and refusing to restructure the Party itself. He stayed in Moscow and fought for Russia's interests against the "dictatorship of the centre". In June 1991 Yeltsin was elected president of Russia, which was a newly created post.

On television, our *zemlyak* appeared larger than life, confident, his stance determined. The reporter explained that Yeltsin considered the actions of the Emergency Committee to amount to a putsch and called for a political strike against them. I had never heard the word "putsch" before and marvelled at the trouble that one syllable had caused. The White House (Russia's main government building, now housing the Duma), the makeshift barricades and the tanks provided a spectacular theatre, surreal in the context of what I had previously seen on TV.

It was Yeltsin who defied the conspirators, distributed flyers and called on Muscovites to come out and protest. Yeltsin's brave resolve, passion and seemingly boundless energy were infectious. Not only his *zemlyaki*, but all of Russia, including the hard-to-please Muscovites, accepted Yeltsin as their saviour. Soldiers defected to support him. Within just two days the putsch was thwarted and its instigators arrested. Gorbachev, who had been held under house arrest in the Crimea, came back to Moscow and yielded greater power to the Soviet republics and Russia in particular. Yeltsin wasted no time. He banned all the Party activities in Russia. He restored the old Russian tricolour flag, which suddenly appeared everywhere. In early September, just after we had started back at school, my hometown Sverdlovsk was rechristened by its original name, Ekaterinburg, in honour of Catherine, the wife of Peter the Great. Leningrad was renamed St. Petersburg once again. Between August and December 1991 ten former republics declared independence from the Soviet Union. Yeltsin secretly met with the leaders of Ukraine and Belarus, and they agreed to form the Commonwealth of Independent

States. On December 25th, Gorbachev resigned as President of the USSR, and that night the red flag was lowered from its mast above the Kremlin, leaving the Russian tricolour. The USSR, replaced by the new Commonwealth, ceased to exist.

That New Year season, along with zesty scent of mandarins, which are always plentiful in Russian shops during the winter, there was a certain whiff of hope in the air, with history and the calendar simultaneously turning a new leaf. The New Year season in Russia is the most festive period of the year, starting at the very end of December and continuing well into January. This is when fir trees are decorated with fairy lights and delicate shiny trinkets to guide *Ded Moroz* (Father Frost) to a safe place to leave his presents at midnight on New Year's Eve. Each city always builds at least one ice park for the children with a giant fir tree, rides carved from ice and fairy-tale figures sculptured from snow. In Ekaterinburg, the city administration organises winter festivities in the central square, right next to the statue of Lenin. The once beloved leader appears to be turning his head to look at the sparkling tree, which dwarfs him in height for a fortnight each year.

The Russian New Year's Eve is thick with traditions. It is quite impossible to imagine a festive table without the *Olivier* salad. In the West, this is often known as "Russian Salad", but it is rarely more than a poor imitation of the classic homemade New Year's dish. First masses of potatoes, carrots and eggs are boiled and peeled. Then these vegetables are diced along with white onions, pickled cucumbers and a generous helping of home-cooked meat or, in its absence, shop-bought boiled *kolbasa* (ham). The only brand good enough to earn its place on the festive table is *Doktorskaya kolbasa* (doctor's ham).

As the name suggests, this brand, invented back in 1936, was marketed as a healthy product, well suited to the Soviet citizens who "wrecked their health, as a result of the Civil War and tsar's despotism", as Anastas Mikoyan, the then People's Commissar of the Food Industries, said. According to the state-issued recipe, *Doktorskaya kolbasa* contained nothing but natural ingredients: beef, lean pork, eggs, milk, salt, sugar and nutmeg. The final ingredient of the *Olivier* salad is tinned peas, a household staple despite their murky green colour. Of course, this substantial salad is dressed with mayonnaise "Provençal".

It took the whole of New Year's Eve to prepare the feast, especially because the celebrations usually lasted for two days and the *Olivier* salad, for one, tasted best the following day. The second ritual complemented the first. Every year Russians watch the two-part romantic comedy *The Irony of Fate (Ironiya Sud'by ili s Legkim Parom!)*, which first came out in 1976. In the film, a young man called Zhenya goes to a public *banya* (sauna) in Moscow with his best friends, as is their New Year's Eve tradition, and everyone gets very drunk. One of his friends is supposed to fly to Leningrad that night, but things get mixed up and Zhenya ends up on the plane instead. Waking up in Leningrad but believing he is in Moscow, Zhenya gets into a taxi, gives the driver his home address and falls asleep. Most streets in Russia have the same names; the standard Soviet architecture produced identical tower blocks with standard door locks. Zhenya gets 'home' and falls asleep. The real owner, the beautiful Nadya, arrives home to find a strange man on her sofa. The rest of the story is painfully funny as Nadya's fiancé throws a tantrum, Zhenya's fiancée in Moscow breaks up with him and the entire New Year's night turns into a tragicomedy with a romantic happy ending. The premiere of *The Irony of Fate* on January 1st 1976 attracted about 100 million viewers. Since then, it's become a tradition to watch the film while chopping ingredients for the *Olivier*.

Finally, no celebration goes ahead without *Sovetskoe Shampanskoye*, the Soviet sparkling wine. In 1924, the Soviet government tasked Russian wine-makers to devise a recipe for a sparkling wine which would be cheap, quick to produce and accessible to the working masses. The new brand, *Sovetskoe Shampanskoye*, was created in 1928. The 'father' of the new drink was Anton Frolov-Bagreyev, a former employee of Prince Golitsyn at Abrau-Dyurso. Prince Golitsyn was a successful winemaker whose sparkling wine, *Novy Svet*, defeated all the French entries and won the Grand Prix de Champagne at the international fair in Paris in 1900. According to some sources, Stalin tasted *Sovetskoe Shampanskoye* in 1942 and declared it a little too sour. Since then, the sparkling wine has been mass-produced as "*demi-brut*" and become a staple feature of any festivity. At midnight, Russians switch on the TV to listen to the speech of their current leader and make wishes to the chiming of the clock of the Kremlin's Spasskaya Tower, before clinking their glasses and drinking *Sovetskoe Shampanskoye*.

In December 1991 we were about to break the tradition and skip the sacred rituals for the first time. We were going to *zagranitsa*! My father had booked us on a New Year cruise in the Baltic Sea and we were to visit Finland, Denmark and Germany, departing from St. Petersburg. To put it into context, most of the people I knew had never been to *zagranitsa* and even if they had, they had only visited the 'friendly' Eastern European countries, such as Bulgaria, Czechoslovakia or Yugoslavia. My grandparents had been to Yugoslavia and my parents had been to Finland just before I was born, but Soviet citizens were chaperoned during such trips and weren't permitted to explore on their own. A tour of Helsinki, for example, would usually be limited to visits to the places where Lenin had stayed while plotting the Revolution. I certainly never met anyone who had been to Britain or the USA. On the way to St. Petersburg, I remember feeling excited but also frightened at the prospect of stepping into a world I could not quite imagine, thanks to the limited information that had been permitted to trickle through to us.

St. Petersburg in December is a gloomy and inhospitable place, tormented by winds and covered in darkness for eighteen hours a day. With its bright interiors and snug cabins, the ship at once offered a luxurious contrast. Our cabin was small and basic, but in the saloon modestly well-off families could mingle with the truly prosperous: mostly overweight men, accompanied by beautiful, young wives and intense-looking bodyguards with flattop hair. In the early 1990s fashion in Russia was as confused as anything else. Men often wore black turtlenecks and sometimes even tracksuit bottoms instead of trousers. Many wore gold chains and bracelets, their thickness intended to signify wealth, not a lack of taste. Women dressed like birds of paradise, combining bright colours in a garish way, desperate to stand out and banish the memories of grey, sombre Soviet uniforms. During that time fashion was frantic, and style elusive. Like a hungry person who gladly eats anything put in front of him, the new Russians anxiously consumed Western clothes, though their hunger was never quite satisfied. The public on our ship dressed up every night to dazzle and impress, filling the dining room with bright silks and feathers, Siberian diamonds and mink furs.

Our first stop was Helsinki. In the Soviet days, a representative of the Communist Party would make a speech, instructing tourists to stay together, follow the tour leader and be mindful of the dangers of the capitalist world they would be stepping into. We were merely warned to return to the ship on time. During the morning tour our guide led us to the statue of Lenin, but then swiftly moved on to show us the fish market, Helsinki's churches and the central boulevard dotted with shops. I was startled by how clean the streets were, as if polished especially for our arrival. All the cars were foreign-made and also clean, despite it being winter. After the tour my parents and I found a Christmas market, with stalls laden with freshly baked cakes and buns, an inconceivable variety of cheese and ham, fresh vegetables and exotic fruit. I was stunned to see bananas displayed in abundance in the middle of winter. Bananas, which appeared in Soviet stores just a couple of times a year during the summer, were the most sought after fruit, and therefore revered by children. Baba Tonya, my grandmother, who lived near a fruit and vegetable store, would queue for hours just to get a kilo of green bananas in order to treat each of her grandchildren once they ripened. In Helsinki the bananas were perfectly yellow and I could not take my eyes off them. My father handed me a couple of coins and told me to buy whatever I wanted. I was briefly seduced by the smell of candied nuts and the cake stand, but I was terrified at the prospect of not having enough money to pay for my treat. I was also anxious about speaking English outside the classroom. The lady selling fruit appeared friendly and I approached her tentatively. My eyes must have told her everything she needed to know: the years of scarcity, and stupor at the sudden abundance, the timidity of a child with her parents just behind her. I handed her my coins and whispered "Bananas…", entirely forgetting the elaborate phrase I'd recited in my mind just seconds earlier. The lady smiled at me and handed me a large bunch of fruit, instantly intoxicating me with its sweet, exotic smell. When I turned around to look at my parents, I was beaming.

In Copenhagen we found a sweet shop where customers were allowed to pick treats they wanted and then pay for them at the till. The concept was so alien to me, I walked round and round the shop with a paper bag, until my father finally took it upon himself to fill it with sweets. The shopkeeper, who looked just like Father Frost with a red nose and a white beard, winked at me and gave me a free lolly. My father then asked me to choose an ice cream from an extraordinary display of flavours, not just chocolate or Plombir. Bewildered by choice, I stood there overwhelmed, stuck to the glass display, like a rubber toy. Eventually, I asked for chocolate.

In Germany we visited Lübeck and Hamburg, where on a sunny winter's day we walked along the marina, which was full of private boats, beautiful cafés with poinsettias on each table and the locals promenading with tiny dogs in matching outfits. By the third landing I became pretty proficient at finding ice cream and sweet stores. Every day I ate a banana, looking forward to telling my grandmother about my bourgeois lifestyle. I was no longer shy but ravenous to take it all in. My first impressions of *zagranitsa* were perfectly shaped apples, each wrapped in paper, surreally tidy streets and infinite choice. My father was taking it in too.

"If you want this plenty, you have to work hard, my daughter", he said in his formal voice, as we were walking back to the ship about to embark on the journey home.

***

It was at a school English contest a couple of years later that I was able to prove myself. I had recovered well after the traumatic interview involving "ships" and "sheep" and had been learning English with gusto. We began English lessons in the first year of school, learning to read and write in English and in Russian at the same time. By year seven, we had seven forty-five minute lessons of English a week. For these lessons we were split into three smaller groups with about twelve pupils in a class. Each lesson typically started with the review of homework, with one pupil coming up to the blackboard to recite a story about a trip to the cinema or sightseeing in London, using new words we'd recently learned. I still remember the beginning of the "cinema story" which began with "I am a great cinema goer..." The rest depended on ability: some pupils just learned the story by heart, others were confident enough to include a personal touch. Only a good story with impeccable pronunciation and grammar earned a top mark. Speaking in front of the class never seemed intimidating since we practised it all the time. Then we would study treacherous irregular verbs and multiple English tenses, which were so different from the simple

Russian "past", "present" and "future". Of course, we learned British English: there were no pants, elevators or eggplants in our vocabulary.

My teacher, Elena Aleksandrovna, who taught me for ten years, had never been abroad. Very few teachers had. Elena Aleksandrovna was of that indeterminate age – older than my parents but not yet close to retirement – which commanded instinctive respect, at least among younger schoolchildren. All the teachers at the prestigious school No. 70 were of that age and they were all women. Elena Aleksandrovna was small and round like a Fabergé egg in a smart suit and heels. She dyed her short, permed hair chestnut red and usually wore plum-coloured lipstick, which she reapplied before each class. Her English was effortlessly British, clear and pure in a way that inspired rather than inflamed professional envy among less able colleagues. Elena Aleksandrovna had studied at the Ural Pedagogical Institute (now the Ural State Pedagogical University) and was assigned a job as a teacher at the school No. 70, the only job which would appear on her curriculum vitae, if she ever wrote one. Like all academics, engineers, doctors and teachers of that time, she was part of the Russian *intelligentsia*: widely read and well educated, regularly visiting the opera house and the theatre, and watching educational programmes on television, which, in any case, dominated the daily schedule. During break times at school she often promenaded along the corridors with her colleague Ludmila Veniaminovna, another English teacher, who had distinctive lilac hair. The pair would not have looked out of place in Baden-Baden. The only crack on Elena Aleksandrovna's otherwise impeccable veneer was her weakness for sweets called Rachki or "little crayfish", which had no association with seafood other than in their name. She treated herself to one sweet during the break between the double lessons, for some reason smoothing out the wrapper on the table before putting it in the bin. Her other unlikely passion was table tennis. Sometimes she played a game or two in the corridor at the end of the school day, still wearing heels and regularly beating her opponents.

It was sometime in autumn 1993 when Elena Aleksandrovna told us about a contest of English to be held at our school among senior pupils. We were to have a written grammar test, an audio comprehension exercise and an oral exam. Each participant had to tell a story about sightseeing in London and to recite a poem in front of a panel of judges, which comprised all the English teachers. Only five students from each year would be declared winners and the prize was unimaginable: a trip to London. "I would be very surprised and disappointed if none of my students won," said Elena Aleksandrovna, as if to no one in particular. I was one of her best students and took up the thinly veiled challenge at once. Who would not want to go to London? I did well in all the tests and won a place, as much because of my proficiency in English as my desire not to let my teacher down.

The trip was organised by our head-teacher, who in the new era of openness and economic opportunities, got in touch with Cator Park School (now Harris Academy) in Bromley, a suburb of London. They worked out an exchange programme which made it possible for a group of students from our school to visit Britain. We were to live with students' families and enjoy sightseeing in London, organised by our partner school. But even without factoring in food and accommodation, travelling to Britain was expensive. I was lucky that my parents could afford to pay for the flights and even give me some pocket money. The parents of another winner from the senior year had to sell their fridge and borrow money from friends to send their son Borya to London. Borya was not popular in his class, and was often teased for his geekiness and his monobrow. After the trip to London, his classmates shunned him altogether for being clever, lucky, or both. Another girl from my year won a place as well, but her parents did not have the money to send her. Her place was taken by a runner-up in more fortunate circumstances. Of course, there was always room to join the trip *po blatu* (using connections), and so the headmaster's son was one of the lucky few to go on the first ever trip to *zagranitsa* from my school.

In early December 1993 we travelled to Moscow on a train, then flew to London with Aeroflot, which gently eased us into the unknown: some passengers on the plane spoke English but the tray food looked unmistakably Russian. In Heathrow we were picked up by our host families and the nightmare began. At thirteen, I was quietly confident about my English but that December night I was just quiet. My exchange pal Kelly had dark hair tied into a tight ponytail, which made her face look unfairly long. She wore glasses and a checked shirt, which looked casual, but must have taken hours to decide on. Kelly sat in the front of the car with her grandfather, who was driving us to Bromley. She chatted incessantly, repeating the words "take that", and yet not offering anything. She asked me lots of questions but I could understand very little. Kelly wore braces, which perhaps made it more difficult, but it did not make me feel better. I was in a state of panic. Kelly was eating sweets and I wanted one too. I was hungry after the uninspiring plane food, as anyone who had travelled with Aeroflot would understand. I found my voice: "Excuse me, Kelly, can I have a sweet?" The subtleties of "can" and "may" would take me years to recognise but I got my sugar fix and broke the language barrier.

Kelly's grandfather took us to Wimpy. It was a special occasion, of course, and Kelly, for one, was excited. She told me all about burgers, including the spicy bean variety, and when the waiter came to our table, she ordered for me as well. I was grateful because I was having a hard time processing the bright interior with an abundance of red plastic, the noisy, happy families around us and the menu options. I had heard of a burger but I'd never seen, let alone eaten one. Fries were another food I only pretended to be familiar with. The actual dinner, when it arrived, was very strange. I tried the squishy bun, the yellow square which must have been cheese, the compressed brown meat, and said I was too tired to eat after the long journey. At least my hosts did not feel obliged to offer me any alcohol, unlike another family, who welcomed my friend Olga (who had just turned fourteen) with a bottle of wine and profuse apologies that they did not have any vodka.

Over the next week Kelly's mum cooked us one scrumptious bowl of spaghetti with creamy sauce, and otherwise we had cereal with milk or 'ready meals'. During our daily excursions to London we received packed lunches, which consisted of a sandwich, a bag of crisps and a small Kit-

Kat. Sandwiches were *triangular* in shape and their fillings were often inedible: "tuna mayonnaise" seemed particularly offensive. But tuna was palatable in comparison with "salt and vinegar" crisps. The greasy slices of potato smelled of spoilt pickles. Once we were invited to the Cator Park School canteen, where we could choose food from a hot buffet with gammon, roast potatoes, fish in batter, chips and peas. Most English students just had chips. To me they did not look appetising and could not compare to mum's pan-fried potatoes. And so every night I went to bed hungry, except for the one time when I managed to pop into a corner shop and buy an extra-large Snickers bar to eat in my room after dinner. When I got back to Russia ten days later, my babushka nearly fainted to see me so thin.

Food aside, London took my breath away. From the bitterly cold, snow-clad Ekaterinburg I was transported into a magical set, trimmed with real green grass lawns in the middle of winter. All the streets were decorated for Christmas but it felt like it had all been done especially for us. In just one week we climbed to the Whispering Gallery of St. Paul's Cathedral, snapped the guards at the Tower of London and Downing Street, went on day trips to Brighton and to Canterbury. One month earlier I had been telling a fictional story about sightseeing in London and now here I was, staring at the real clock face of Big Ben. During a tour of the Houses of Parliament I sat down on a well-worn green leather bench of the Commons Chamber and was asked by the guide: "What is the name of our Prime Minister?" I thought he was asking my name and replied "Yana Bakunina!". I stood corrected, for it was, of course, John Major, who did not quite pique my interest. John Major did not inspire the same admiration the Russians felt for his predecessor, Margaret Thatcher. We reached every corner of Hyde Park, chased every squirrel along The Mall and fought the pigeons for access to the Nelson's Column in Trafalgar Square. We shamelessly stole pens and pencil sharpeners from the National Portrait Gallery souvenir shop because we had never come across such 'honest' shops before. We were mesmerised by the advertising at Piccadilly Circus, like magpies attracted by shiny trinkets. We tirelessly trudged through the crowds on Oxford Street, buying presents for our families and ourselves. I bought a black plastic keyring with the slogan "London – Capital of the World" and chanted it to myself at bedtime.

I came back to Russia with a tin of Quality Street chocolates for Elena Aleksandrovna and a dream that I would one day live in London. My host Kelly never made it to Russia (travel was too expensive), but I'm certain that she too kept a few memories of a strange Russian girl who had never heard of Take That.

Chapter V in which I learned German

In the early 1990s, Russia's president Boris Yeltsin and his team introduced radical economic reforms. They removed state regulation of prices, which led to a threefold increase in the cost of food and other staples, the market values of which had been previously suppressed amid widespread shortages. Hyperinflation quickly wiped out people's nominal savings. Salaries were delayed and many pensioners found themselves begging or selling anything they had at makeshift market stalls: homemade jams, pickles and even Second World War medals...

The voucher privatisation, which was announced under the slogans of inclusion and justice and offered 148 million people the opportunity to exchange state-issued vouchers for shares in the newly privatised enterprises, was no more than a PR scam. Most people, confused by the new terminology and distrustful of the government, exchanged their vouchers for bottles of vodka or invested in mutual funds which sprang up and disappeared overnight. Two thirds of all state assets were sold at private auctions and ended up in the hands of the few.

The 1990s are remembered in Russia for hyperinflation, the rise of organised crime and the emergence of oligarchs.

Ekaterinburg and Ratingen, Germany, 1994

"Sergey Aleksandrovich, I see that you drive an *inomarka* (imported car)..." said Alla Sergeevna, my Russian literature teacher, her tone ingratiating, her eyes darting from my father's car, parked outside, to his suit and coat. "We could really do with a video cassette player for our classroom. I'd like to show the students some scenes from the film adaptation of *War and Peace* they'll be reading in their final year..."

Alla Sergeyevna, who was in her fifties, looked like she belonged to a different era in her vintage dresses and the traditional white shawl of fine Orenburg wool that usually covered her shoulders. She always wore the same drop earrings, made with what was unmistakeably "Russian gold", which looks reddish, blended with copper. Alla Sergeyevna's bleached bob and pearly pink lipstick made her look ludicrous. She was enthralled by Russian literature and its timeless heroes. The object of her passions would switch from Griboyedov's Chatsky to Dostoevsky's Raskol'nikov in a matter of a school term. Her infatuation with Golden Age literature was particularly infectious. I was captivated by Pushkin, Dostoevsky and especially Tolstoy. But the real world Alla Sergeyevna lived in was brutal. She was an esteemed teacher in a prestigious school, but her status did not translate into having a meal on the table every night. With the ever rising prices, Alla Sergeyevna could not afford much with her salary, and she was not the only teacher to appeal to the pupils' parents for help.

"You know, Yana is very likely to get a gold medal of distinction at the end of school, with her academic record..." she said meaningfully.

My father, who had come to pick me up after school, saw a desperate woman he could not help. "Alla Sergeyevna, it is exactly because of Yana's academic record that I won't help you. She will get that gold medal all by herself. I'm afraid you've approached the wrong parent."

Not everyone was as proud as my father. The new money afforded new opportunities to parents who could now circumvent the entrance requirements to get their children into good schools or attempt to influence their marks. Soon Alla Sergeyevna played us her favourite episodes from *War and Peace*, based on Tolstoy's epic novel. She sat at her desk, wrapped in her shawl, and watched Natasha Rostova making her formal debut at a high society ball. By contrast, her fourteen-year-old students fidgeted, not at all impressed with the black-and-white scenes, which paled in comparison to the Bruce Lee action films that were now available via subscription. Every night an entrepreneurial cable channel, launched in Ekaterinburg, showed two films of dubious quality, filmed at the back of a cinema somewhere in the US. The Russian voiceover was deliberately nasal to disguise its source – but he needn't have worried; piracy laws were not enforced in the 1990s.

Similarly, the *War and Peace* ball gowns were pretty but not as exciting as the sassy dresses on the fashion pages of *Cosmopolitan*, the first glossy Western magazine published in Russia in May 1994. It was expensive but my friend Anya had a copy. A supermodel called Cindy Crawford was on the cover, wearing a tight and revealing black dress, her luxuriant hair cascading down her shoulders. *"Sex or chocolate? Everything in good time!"* one headline reassured us. *"Thirty-something, independent, confident... Do they need a husband?"* another asked. Anya and her friend Masha sat with the magazine on their laps, slowly flicking the pages under the cover of their desk. Natasha Rostova had no chance against Cindy Crawford. I looked around the classroom. Instead of school uniform (which had been abolished) my classmates now wore mini-skirts, flannel shirts and flared jeans. In the Soviet days there had been no brands on offer in Russia, but in the 1990s tons of fake designer clothes were brought over from Istanbul's bazaars. Genuine European brands became available too and soon our classroom was no longer a sea of brown and navy blue. Our wardrobes sprouted many new colours but the two most telling shades were rich and poor, reflecting the relative fortunes of our parents.

During breaks between lessons some pupils talked about downhill skiing and lawn tennis, while others experimented with smoking behind the school building. Anya and Masha would conspire to go to a gig at Sphinx. It was a new bar and music venue, known as "the centre of rock" and the coolest place in Ekaterinburg, where local and touring rock bands played on Friday nights. I was gossiping about a handsome final-year student with my new friend Olga, with whom I had bonded on the trip to London. Other classmates were preoccupied with the imminent choice they had to make either to leave school after eight years or stay for two more years in order to apply to university. But regardless of our circumstances, we were all shielded by our school and its demanding teachers from the anarchy outside its walls.

Walking alone in the dark was no longer safe. Women took off their earrings on the way home from work to avoid having their earlobes torn by merciless street robbers. On public transport everyone clung to their bags which were often cut off and pilfered during rush hour. My mother was robbed on the street, her bag and fur hat snatched by a common thief, who took off before she remembered the tear gas spray in her coat pocket. Like many others, we installed a second door at the entrance to our flat to keep out burglars. The ubiquitous kiosks at bus stops, which sold imported chocolate and cigarettes, were now governed by the newly formed mafia bands, which collected 'protection' money from powerless vendors. On the local news, our screens were overwhelmingly filled with stories of rape and murder. A so-called "gypsy village", just a few minutes' walk from our school, became one of the city's drug hotspots. I frequently saw used needles lying on the side of the pavements on my way home. Yet somehow my mind was doggedly preoccupied with algebra, Russian literature and history.

My family too protected me from the chaos of the early 1990s. The fall of the Soviet Union was excruciatingly painful for my grandfather, whose career was centred around the achievements of Leninist ideology. But he coped by throwing himself into his work. Aleksandr Bakunin got access to the newly opened archives and began researching the evolution of totalitarian power in the Soviet Union. In 1994 he published an article, *The Genesis of Soviet Totalitarianism,* in an academic journal and began writing a trilogy, *The History of Soviet Totalitarianism,* looking especially at the mass repressions in the Urals. Auntie Natasha and my mother joined my father's firm. Uncle Borya became head of the Politics faculty of the Ural State University. Politics was a new subject, and my uncle helped to develop the curriculum. Their son, my cousin Dima, took up karate just as martial arts became popular in Russia, thanks to kung-fu films and the new street crime. Many took up self-defence classes in the face of neighbourhood gangs and opportunistic robbers. While my grandfather was reading about Stalin and my cousin was practising his karate chop, I was learning German.

It was my father's idea. He had business partners in Leipzig, Hamburg and Düsseldorf and was already thinking about my future. At school we had begun learning a second foreign language in addition to English. At that time French was only deemed useful insofar as it enabled you to read a letter at the beginning of the *War and Peace*. German was considered a more pragmatic choice. In the 1990s when thousands of employees of defunct state enterprises were laid off, practical knowledge – English, German, mathematics, computer science – was favoured over history and literature. Most of my classmates and I chose German, but with just two lessons a week, we did not learn very much during the first term. After the New Year break, my father decided to hire me a private tutor. It was uncle Borya who helped him find one and introduced us to his colleague.

Galina Isaakovna was head of Foreign Languages at the Ural State University (now part of the merged UrFU). She was a birdlike woman in her late sixties, if I were to guess, with a neat grey bob and thick glasses, which magnified her kind eyes. Galina Isaakovna looked deceptively like an indulgent grandmother, but in reality she was strict, and I was her glutton for punishment. Her husband had already retired and received a meagre pension; Galina Isaakovna held an important position at the university but even so her salary must have been pitiful. Up until *perestroika* she had lived in a world where making a profit or money on the side was considered a sin, but in the 1990s many university teachers began private tutoring, which made a substantial difference to their lives.

Twice a week after school, I took a tram to the university, which stood opposite the Ekaterinburg Theatre of Opera and Ballet. The theatre is a magnificent white ornate building, resembling a giant meringue cake, built back in 1912. Inside, it always seemed another world with burgundy velvet draping and golden interior decorations. Women, coming to see a ballet, always dressed up and brought a change of shoes in winter in order to fit in with the rich surroundings. I still remember a white wool dress embroidered with pale flowers, which I wore when I went to see my first ballet, *Swan Lake*. The university was grey and solemn by comparison, but equally intimidating. The man checking passes at the entrance looked too intelligent for his menial job, and angry rather than grateful for having one. He would bark at me, then relax upon hearing Galina Isaakovna's name, like a guard dog suddenly tamed by catching a whiff of its master.

Galina Isaakovna insisted on addressing me in German and only switching to Russian to translate a word or explain a grammatical rule. Her office was cold, with the state-funded central heating no longer reliable. The German language too seemed frosty at first. It was frustrating to grapple with German articles, which differed according to gender and often didn't correspond to the Russian equivalents. *Mädchen*, a girl, has a neutral, rather than a feminine gender in German, and so does a hen (*Huhn*). Galina Isaakovna had no mercy and drilled me fastidiously, completely oblivious to my complaints about being overloaded with homework.

"Muss is eine harte Nuss", she'd say, looking at me through her thick lenses and nodding at my exercise book.

"That's another proverb I'll have to look up!" I'd reply, fuming.

At home it turned out the proverb translated as "in for a penny, in for a pound". My tutor was right about me.

Little by little, I was getting to grips with the language. German is easy enough to read and write, with vastly fewer exceptions to the rules than in Russian or English. Its vocabulary is also simpler, with many words built up from common roots. "*Tuch*" means "kerchief", "cloth"; "*Handtuch*" is a "hand towel"; "*Betttuch*" means a "bed sheet"; "*Halstuch*" is a "neck tie". Still, the new language sounded dry and bitter to me in comparison to my already fluent English.

Galina Isaakovna also taught a weekly evening class in conversational German. I joined those classes, which were attended by some particularly ambitious students, who had come to realise that a foreign language was an asset worth having. We were taught with a method developed by the Soviet academic Igor Shekhter, who in the 1970s came up with a sensory and emotive approach to teaching foreign languages. The method consisted of learning new phrases and repetition, dipping into the culture of the foreign language, reciting poems and singing songs, with the learning taking place at the subconscious level. Singing was Galina Isaakovna's passion. We sang our hearts out every lesson, building up a healthy repertoire of German and Austrian songs. My favourite was a tongue twister about a maiden called Lies, who is looking forward to a visit by Hans and wondering if he will arrive via Oberammergau, or Unterammergau, or if he will come at all:

Heut kommt der Hans zu mir,
Freut sich die Lies.
Ob er aber über Oberammergau,
Oder aber über Unterammergau,
Oder aber überhaupt nicht kommt,
Ist nicht gewiss.

I was careful not to mention to my friends that I was becoming rather fond of singing folk songs. German too became less of a stranger and more of a friend.

After lessons I went to the bus stop to go back home, enviously watching people unburdened by homework, who would meet by the brightly lit opera theatre. The journey would take about an hour in a tightly packed bus full of angry, weary people returning from work. Getting a seat or even claiming enough space to open a book was a luxury. Sometimes I would take a tram and stay overnight at my grandmother's in the centre of the city, by the circus. Baba Tonya was always delighted to see me, which inevitably meant a feast of her scrumptious cooking. More often than not, she would also bake what she called "a sweet pie", despite not having a very sweet tooth herself. She would spread finely chopped fresh apples, wild blueberries and loganberries, preserved in sugar, on a flat sheet of pastry and bake it until the fruit and the berries caramelised. She liked her sweet pie cold with a cup of hot tea. After dinner, I would stay in the kitchen to do my homework. Babushka would retire to the living room to watch her beloved Mexican soap opera, *Prosto Mariya* (*Simplemente Maria*).

Latin American soap operas flooded Russian television

and acquired millions of fans, especially among the older generation. At first my grandmother lived for *Escrava Isaura* (A Slave Called Isaura), about a poor mixed-race girl struggling against the injustices of her class in nineteenth-century Brazil. For the next few years Baba Tonya empathised with Mexican Maria, a beautiful peasant girl who came to a city to find work and fell in love with the rich Juan Carlos, who abandoned her as soon as he found out that she was pregnant. Maria then breaks through to become a famous fashion designer and sends her son to study law. At university he meets a girl, who inevitably is revealed to be related to him, and the plot thickens, involving a shooting, death in childbirth and merciless family drama, hardly appropriate entertainment for faint-hearted pensioners. Still, the soaps provided a much-needed respite from the rising crime, inflation and political pandemonium of real life. The only thing Babushka had no patience for when watching TV was the adverts.

Ads were new for the Russians. This made them undoubtedly effective. The general lawlessness of the 1990s was reflected on TV screens, with advertising appearing at a greater sound volume than the programmes and promoting openly dubious ventures. From the kitchen I could hear the familiar jovial music of the MMM commercial. Its protagonist, Lyenya Golubkov, was a simpleton, a common Russian man wearing an *ukhanka* fur hat with floppy ears, who was trying his luck at capitalism by investing in shares of MMM. Just two weeks later, he had made enough money to buy his wife a pair of winter boots. In the next instalment of the ad, Lyenya bought his wife a fur coat and was planning to buy a car the following month. MMM was allegedly such a profitable venture that in just a few months Lyenya could buy a house in Paris. In fact MMM was a pyramid scheme, promising 1000% returns, and its television campaign was highly successful, targeting the simple folks. My grandmother prudently kept her "funeral fund", as she had referred to her savings, in a tin under her bed, not least because she disliked Lyenya Golubkov's wife, a plump, dumb-witted lady who was continuously eating expensive chocolates straight from the box. Unlike my sensible grandmother, fifteen million people in Russia were conned by MMM in early 1990s.

Once school was over that year, my friends dispersed for the three months of summer holidays. Many went to summer camps, which were previously called "pioneer camps" and now simply "camps". No longer subsidised by state enterprises or government institutions, these camps became unaffordable for many families. On the other hand, elite camps on the Black Sea, which were previously only open to children of the party *nomenklatura* or the KGB officers, now targeted the offspring of entrepreneurs. That summer my classmates Anya and Masha went to Orlyenok ("eaglet"), a famous seaside camp, which used to line up children each morning for a briefing on communist ideals and then hold a range of compulsory educational and sporting activities throughout the day. In 1994 Anya and Masha spent most of their daytime on the beach, and in the evenings they were entertained by the local boys playing music by the sea.

My summer was less relaxing. Unlike my friends, I stayed in Ekaterinburg. Four days a week I went to Galina Isaakovna's flat near the cinema, one with a striking name *Burevestnik* (thunderbird), for my German lessons in the afternoon. In the mornings I did my homework. I hardly saw my parents, who spent their summer evenings at the *dacha* and drove back to Ekaterinburg for work. Mum would pop in to cook me some food and give me pocket money. I remember being completely immersed in my studies, not without some resentment, but I did not have time to sulk. Galina Isaakovna, who looked even more relaxed at home with her flowery tablecloth and pot plants, was enjoying herself at my expense. She treated me as an experiment and kept poking me with grammar and new words. She was a happy professor receiving a generous grant for a far-fetched study. *"Sehr gut, Jana. Bis Morgen!"* (Very good, Yana, see you tomorrow!), she would say at the end of each day and I could see her already plotting a new form of torture for me. There was a supermarket across the road from Galina Isaakovna's, and right next to it old women used to assemble a makeshift market, selling fresh herbs grown at their *dacha* plots, wild strawberries picked early in the morning, and flowers. I often bought berries from them to eat on the bus home. *"Vnuchen'ka, kupi tsvetochki!"* (Granddaughter, buy some flowers!), they implored me, not because they were seasoned hustlers, but because they were desperate.

My nightly reward was to watch MTV, which had recently appeared on cable and instantly captivated Russian teenagers. Before MTV launched their Russian version of the music channel playing both Russian and English songs, we watched the American version, and for the first time we fell in love with the same songs as youngsters in the US. That June it was the song *Crazy* by Aerosmith which became my obsession. I could have watched Alicia Silverstone and Liv Tyler on repeat (if only we had owned a video recorder), savouring every moment of the openly provocative story of two schoolgirls, skipping school, exploring their sexuality and even entering an amateur pole-dancing competition. By fourteen, my blonde hair grew down to my shoulders, and I wanted to be Alicia – beautiful, playful and carefree. Instead, I persevered with my crash course in German. By the end of July, I was ready.

***

In early August we hosted a family party at our flat. It was unusual to gather in the city rather than at the *dacha* in the summer, but the occasion was special: I was departing for Germany where I would stay until Christmas with the family of one of my father's business partners. I would attend the same school as his children, practise German and get a taste of European education. We assembled in the living room, which had been completely renovated with new embossed wallpaper, plush light teal sofa and armchairs, new cabinets and a dining table. Unlike our previous dark furniture and sombre grey textiles, the new look was softer and aspiring to feel European. My father had bought a painting by the renowned local artist Mikhail Sazhaev and a Russian Orthodox icon, which now hung in the corner of the room. My father and I had been christened a few years earlier when I was ten and he was thirty-five. My mother had been christened at birth and now wore a small cross on a delicate golden chain around her neck. Christianity became fashionable, and our new icon was more of a tribute to the changing times than a display of newly found faith.

My grandfather thought as much and cocked his eyebrow at the sight of the Virgin Mary, but said nothing. His mind was occupied with the speech he was about to deliver. He stood up at the head of the table and cleared his throat. His wife Lena, his children, Natasha and Sergey, my uncle Borya, my mum and her mother, Antonina Fedorovna (my Baba Tonya), all looked up expectantly. "Back in 1945, when the Soviet Army had declared a decisive victory over Nazi Germany, I could not have imagined that some fifty years later my own granddaughter would be on her way to study in West Germany. How times change. Let's drink to peace and the future, especially the future of my granddaughter, Yana, who is making the most of the opportunities now available to the people of Russia." My grandfather's words have stayed with me. It was a display of hard-earned wisdom by the Professor who had come to accept the new times despite the importance of the memory of the Second World War, relentlessly cultivated in the post-war Soviet Union.

The Great Patriotic War, which is how the Second World War is referred to in Russia, was regarded as the most sacred event in our history, partly because it was still fresh in people's memories and partly because it symbolised the triumph of Soviet socialism over the evils of the capitalist West. Soviet films, books and history lessons at school taught us that only a nation strengthened by the ideals of collectivism versus selfish individualism, equality rather than competition, and state rather than private ownership could have mobilised its people to defeat the Third Reich. The novels about the Great Patriotic War were my favourites. Black-and-white films about brave Soviet soldiers, ingenious spies and selfless partisans dominated the TV schedule in the run-up to the May 9th, or Victory Day, celebrated in Russia as a public holiday. My favourite film was *A Zori Sdes' Tikhie* (The Dawns Here Are Quiet), a heart-breaking story about five young women who volunteer to fight in the war in 1942 and are sent to Karelia (near Finland) as trainee snipers. The sergeant major is at first unimpressed with the task of teaching and commanding the new recruits, but in the heat of a sudden unequal battle against sixteen German paratroopers, the girls fight heroically, only to die one-by-one. The heroines are ordinary girls who are both merry and mischievous, and determined and brave until the very end.

Every year Victory Day in Russia is celebrated by a vast military parade, broadcast on national television. It is considered a tradition, a grateful nod to the war veterans rather than a display of power. In the evening, each big Russian city puts on a display of fireworks. Crowds of people always assemble at *Plotinka* (little dam), the centre of Ekaterinburg, where the river Iset' had been dammed to form a large pond. The atmosphere is festive with music, drinks and snacks. Once the sun sets an elaborate kaleidoscope of lights dazzles the skyline. The fireworks too are a traditional spectacle and a communal experience, much like Guy Fawkes Night in Britain.

Before my departure for Germany, the possibility of tension over the shared historic events had not crossed my mind. At fourteen, I fretted over my wardrobe and whether my German was good enough. When mum brought a cake she had baked especially for me, I burst out laughing. It was my favourite homemade cake, which was filled with sour cream, dried apricots, prunes, poppy seeds and walnuts, but its name, like many other Russian delicacies, was simply too peculiar to explain to a foreigner. It was called *Trukhlyavy Pen'* ("a mouldering stump").

***

Alexander von Korff and his family lived in Ratingen, near Düsseldorf in Nordrhein-Westfalen. Alexander's mother had emigrated from Russia after the Bolshevik revolution and was determined to pass on her cultural roots to her descendants. Just like his mother, Alexander spoke fluent Russian. He had studied Slavic and Business in the US, where he met his future wife, Irina, an American with a Russian name. They called their sons Alexei, Alexander (Sandro) and Nicholas. Alexander's business interests took him often to Moscow where he worked as an intermediary between German consumer brands and Russian buyers. The family lived in Ratingen in a large, beautiful, classically decorated house with a proper dining room, a guest bedroom, a library and a garden. It looked so alien to me, I felt as if I had landed on the Moon.

That first day in August we sat down for some afternoon tea with Sandro and Nicholas, who were just back from riding their horses. The family's two black Labradors, Toby and Benz, joined us in the garden. Irina made *Pflaumenstreuselkuchen* (plum crumble cake), and I was embarrassed to realise that during my five-month crash course in German, I had never learned the word plum. Nor was peach part of my curriculum. Innocuous as it may seem, the words "Pflaume" and "Pfirsich" are fiendishly difficult to learn and pronounce because of the offending excess of consonants. Other than that, I fared reasonably well, despite the culture shock. At dinner we used meticulously polished silverware and ate a three-course meal every day. During my stay, I tried avocado, artichokes and green basil for the first time. I gorged on pineapples and grouse, like the proverbial bourgeois. At the same time, I was amazed to see that both men and dogs ate crunchy cereal for breakfast. Alexander and Irina were incredibly kind to me, and patient. I felt relatively at ease with them, rarely turning to English as my safety net. School was another matter.

Suitbertus Gymnasium was a well-respected Catholic secondary school in Kaiserswerth near Düsseldorf. The form master of the class I joined for a term was Herr Ley, a jovial English and French teacher with an enormous moustache, who always smelled of liquorice. He introduced me to the class of about twenty pupils sitting at a horseshoe-shaped table. There was an empty seat near André, the self-consciously laid-back, popular guy with a crop of straw-blond hair and blue eyes. Next to him sat Franka and Julia. Both wore simple yet carefully applied make-up, jeans and fitted tops. Like anyone encountering a foreigner, they spoke to me slowly but without simplifying their vocabulary. Usually the opposite helps, but I appreciated their attention. They looked so effortlessly trendy, and they talked about salsa lessons and boyfriends. I wanted to fit in.

I noticed that no one wore fringes anymore and decided to grow mine out. One day I styled it up with some hair gel I borrowed from Nicholas. The effect resembled the accident in *There's Something About Mary.* As soon as I took my seat that morning, André said helpfully: *"Das ist nicht Mode in Deutschland"* (It's not fashionable in Germany). I could have died of embarrassment.

That particular incident was nothing in comparison to the *kiwigate*. Irina gave me a packed lunch every morning, which included a sandwich, a small carton of juice and a piece of fruit. I went through apples and bananas without causing a diplomatic incident but a kiwi was my downfall. It was only the second time I had seen a kiwi so I ate it – skin and all – in the middle of the schoolyard during a lunch break. The incident was quickly reported to Nicholas, who was a year older than me at the same school. He, in turn, spilled the beans to the family at dinner. "Did you really eat the kiwi with the skin on?" he asked, marvelling at me as if I was an exotic freak from a travelling circus. I desperately wanted to be swallowed by the earth, clutching at the consolation that the word *"Schale"* (skin, peel) was likely to stay imprinted in my mind forever after.

My favourite lesson was English. I was pleased to realise that the Russian school of English had taught me well, and I was easily ahead of my German peers. Herr Ley, the English teacher, also tutored me in German when the rest of the class had their German literature lessons. He usually picked a story for me and sucked on his liquorice sweets while I was reading it aloud. While other teachers kept their distance from me, Herr Ley found me curious and enjoyed the extra responsibility. He even showcased me to his junior English students while my classmates studied Latin, and I would stand up in front of the class and talk about life in Russia. They asked me about Russian food, about snow and bears.

Like any Russian, I could barely resist telling them that in winter bears knocked at people's doors and begged for lumps of sugar.

My nemesis was the biology teacher who spoke an incomprehensible dialect I had no hope of understanding. Even if she had spoken *Hochdeutsch,* the standard German, I had no chance in participating in class in any meaningful way. Galina Isaakovna had not covered photosynthesis. The biology teacher was a woman of principle and at the end of the term she marked my test with *ungenügend*, the lowest possible grade, and pointed out to the entire class that the Russian had only answered one and a half questions right. André, who got *mangelhaft*, a barely better grade, patted me on the back in a spontaneously amiable gesture. We had something in common after all.

By the end of my stay in Ratingen I was sick of packed lunches, German mayonnaise and biology lessons, but I wasn't desperate to go home. I missed my family and friends, I looked forward to showing off my new clothes and jewellery at school, but something held me back. I think it was the constant supply of hot water, the bountiful spread of food in the supermarkets and something else: Alexander's mother reading novels rather than worrying about the price of milk; Julia thinking of studying art rather than aiming for a more profitable profession and the von Korffs ordering pizza when they couldn't be bothered to cook. It was such a carefree world. In comparison, Russia seemed like an obstacle course governed by the survival of the fittest.

Chapter VI in which Lev Tolstoy saved the day

A decade after the promising call for *perestroika*, life in Russia had not lived up to expectations. The economy continued to deteriorate, with many workers going unpaid for months. The gap between rich and poor was widening. Following the parliamentary elections in December 1995, the Communist Party dominated the Duma (the lower house of the Russian parliament, which had replaced the Supreme Soviet in 1993). The standard-bearer for the Communist Party, Gennady Zyuganov, emerged as a strong opposition leader to challenge Yeltsin. Zyuganov criticised the Western ideals which had infiltrated Russian lives. He attacked Yeltsin for patronage and the widespread influence of the oligarchs.

In June 1996, presidential elections were held in Russia, with Yeltsin receiving 35.8% of the votes and Zyuganov coming a close second with 32.5%. In the second round, Yeltsin won with 53.8%. It later emerged that the oligarchs, fearful of the consequences of a communist victory, had made a pact to support Yeltsin's campaign and put their money behind it. It helped that the oligarchs controlled Russia's mass media, which had waged a persuasive war against Zyuganov. The oligarchs' grip on the media was so tight that the nation remained unaware that, with less than a fortnight to go before the second round of elections, Yeltsin had suffered a serious heart attack and could barely function. Yeltsin's victory in 1996 was less about the triumph of democracy and more to do with the business tycoons pulling the necessary strings to stay in power.

Ekaterinburg, 1995-1996

After five months in Germany, I came back to Ekaterinburg and joined my classmates for the second semester of the penultimate year of school. At first everything seemed a little disjointed. Anya and Masha had both dyed their hair chestnut red and were now spending time with their new boyfriends after school. The boys in my class suddenly looked and sounded different. My entire year group was reorganised into classes which specialised in different subjects: mathematics and physics, humanities and natural sciences. I broke Alevtina Aleksandrovna's heart and chose to take more literature and history, rather than maths. The new class formations meant weaning off old friends and making new ones, but we were all equally anxious about the final school year exams and university applications.

Russians have to make up their minds about their future professions at just seventeen when they finish school and enrol in higher education. A typical degree takes five years, and Russian employers look to harvest highly specialised graduates. My generation was especially mindful of applying for a course with good job prospects. Many of my classmates chose to study computer science, economics, management, law and foreign languages. Some had seen their parents being laid off by state enterprises and struggling to adapt to changes. It was unthinkable to study literature or history in the days when previously revered *intelligentsia* appeared out of date, like tins of marrow caviar – a beloved Soviet delicacy now gathering dust at the back of the stores. In the 1990s, former *apparatchiks* were impatient to reinvent themselves as businessmen. Whereas in the Soviet days a trader was looked upon with contempt, in the new age, the emerging breed of *kommersant* (a businessman) with his handful of crisp *zelyenen'kiye* (green; referring to US dollars) became a role model.

In 1996, my graduation year, each school set its own exams, with the exception of maths and Russian literature, which were mandatory for all final year students in Russia. In our school, which specialised in foreign languages, English and either German or French were compulsory too. Soon after the exam results were released, graduates applied to university and had to sit entrance exams just weeks later. By the 1990s universities became commercially savvy and offered paid places along with the free ones. The exams were quite challenging, and the contest for free places was fierce. Universities also organised paid evening courses for prospective students to prepare them for the exams. Such courses were very popular, and some students even travelled to Ekaterinburg from nearby towns every week just to feel more secure about their prospects. I was planning to apply to study international economic relations at the Ural State University of Economics and attended evening maths classes once a week together with several of my former classmates, who had chosen to study advanced maths and physics. It's not that we weren't taught maths well at school, but the university was going to set deliberately different tests to pick the best of the crop and supplement its own income by encouraging the less bright but more financially fortunate students to pay tuition fees.

I was lucky. I had a clean slate of top marks in all subjects at school, which meant that I was excused from sitting school exams, save for the mandatory maths test and a literature essay.

I cruised through the maths test and was looking forward to the literature exam. It was a beautiful, warm and sunny June morning. All the students wore smart white shirts and dark skirts or trousers, resembling a colony of penguins. I arrived early with my hardback volumes of *War and Peace, Crime and Punishment* and *Eugene Onegin.* The books were checked for cheat sheets and deposited at the back of the classroom. The task was to write an essay answering one of the questions based on the novels we had studied in the past two years. We were allowed to use the books for reference during the exams. I was hoping for a good question on *War and Peace* and looked back at my emerald green volumes of Tolstoy's epic. We had six hours to write the essay and weren't allowed to leave the room except to use the toilet. Some of the parents volunteered to come and bring us snacks half way through the exam. Alla Sergeevna, tugging at the ruffle of her blouse, started the clock and wished us luck.

I remember finding a question I liked and setting to work, feeling simultaneously relieved and excited. The trick with the Russian literature exam was to write a draft focussing on the answer before copying it out and scrutinising the text for any spelling or grammar mishaps. I remember racing against the clock to finish copying out my essay. I did not have time for any snacks, and my bladder was about to burst. I made it just in time, dropping my pen and shaking my aching hand. My shirt was clinging to me and my white sleeves were marked with ink blots. I wish I could remember what my essay was about, but such was the intensity that the details elude me to this day. I high-fived my friend Irina who, like me, was a candidate for the medal with her clean slate of top marks. It was our last exam – now we just had to wait for the results.

The school literature essay mattered hugely. We had studied Russian for eight years, finally dropping the subject for the last two years of school. During that time our essays were given two marks: one for content and one for grammar. The exam essay was given just one mark, meaning that *one missing comma* could ruin the fruits of six hours of labour. A "four" (rather than an "five") would mean no gold medal, which was not just a matter of pride. A gold medal was awarded for top marks in all subjects at the end of the final school year *and* in all exams. With a gold medal, I had to take just one entrance exam to get into university. Otherwise, in addition to a maths test, I'd have to write another essay and take oral exams in history and English. I was banking, perhaps somewhat recklessly, on getting that medal and so was preparing only for maths.

It was a shock therefore to discover that I had in fact got a "four" rather than a "five" for my essay. The culprit was a comma, one tiny blue dash, which the examiner had deemed superfluous. Alla Sergeevna offered me some valerian drops (a popular Russian herbal remedy to calm one down), but I wasn't having it.

"I need to appeal!" I cried.

Medal candidates were offered the right to appeal, although in practice appeals rarely succeeded. I received my essay back and stared at the treacherous sentence for an eternity, while my mind searched for a clue that might help me win my case.

"Alla Sergeevna, do you have a copy of *War and Peace*

here?" I asked the teacher, who looked crestfallen. It made me think that her honour was at stake here too.

She gave me an old volume with a creased grey spine and pencil marks in the margins. I began reading the novel again, scanning the pages, looking for a sentence that could save me.

"I found it! Look here, Alla Sergeevna, this sentence is structured just like mine and Tolstoy, Lev Nikolaevich himself, used a comma just like I did! They cannot argue with Tolstoy, can they?"

The appeal process was deliberately intimidating to ensure that not too many were tempted. It was held at the imposing ministry of education in the centre of Ekaterinburg. Alla Sergeevna and I met at the entrance on the morning of the appeal. A line of other hopefuls from all around the city gathered there too. Most of them were accompanied by their parents, although only students and teachers were allowed inside. Alla Sergeevna wore a suit rather than a dress and flat shoes. She looked smaller and completely out of her element. If I had harboured any doubts about it previously, it dawned on me then that the appeal process was down to me alone. I clutched my Tolstoy and put on a brave face, "We'll win this, Alla Sergeevna, don't you worry."

The appeal commission for Russian literature essays comprised a dozen teachers from different schools, gathered in a large room into which the light was streaming through tall windows, blinding the entrants. The setting reminded me of my first ever exam ten years earlier, except that I was no longer a shy duckling urged on by my father. I greeted the three teachers examining my appeal with the supreme confidence I wish I had bottled at sixteen. I sat down, with

Alla Sergeevna taking a chair beside me. I argued my case fluently and with conviction. I read the sentence from *War and Peace*. "Just like Tolstoy, I am fond of long sentences and I used a comma to emphasise my point. It's subjective, I admit, and I am at your mercy, but I believe that my essay deserves a top mark." At that moment, the buzz in the room faded abruptly and everything seemed to play out in slow motion. One of the examiners looked away from me to her colleagues, who gave barely perceptible nods. She looked down at her notes and back up. "Thank you, Yana. You did very well here and your appeal is granted. Congratulations on your gold medal." Alla Sergeevna began to cry. Her handkerchief, I noticed, was embroidered by hand.

***

Our graduation ball took place on June 21st 1996, the week after the first round of Russia's presidential elections. The poster still hanging above the school entrance announced it as a voting station. At that time, it looked like a nuisance, stealing attention away from the school sign, rather than a historic memento. We posed for photos on the steps. Anya, Masha and Natasha wore almost identical short black dresses inspired by Brenda, Kelly and Donna from *Beverley Hills, 90210*. I was wearing a light grey dress with a shimmering bodice and a long flowing skirt. Puffed sleeves were tucked just above my elbows and wrists, completing the dreamy "Natasha Rostova" look. All the girls had spent hours at the hairdressers' and wore elaborate hairstyles. My long blonde hair was put up in rolls and delicate curls, fixed by a gallon of hairspray. I borrowed the dress from a prominent local fashion designer, and my hairdresser was a catwalk stylist.

The fashion industry had blossomed in Ekaterinburg, with catwalk shows being organised as entertainment as well as a statement of couture. The emerging *nouveau riche* often booked designers to host shows in a night club or even on the stage of the opera house to add glamour to corporate parties. The models were encouraged to linger after the shows and mingle with rich men, for whom dating a model was a status symbol (along with a thick gold chain, a large Swiss watch and a Mercedes). The girls did not shy away because often rich, older lovers were their tickets out of poverty. The industry enjoyed unprecedented freedom after *perestroika* with its glamour, late night parties and many openly gay designers and male models. I too worked as a model in my final year of school, glad to be earning pocket money and shedding my tomboy image. After the late catwalks, I was lucky to have my father picking me up and taking me home, away from the bright lights of the predatory cars.

After the formal ceremony in the assembly hall, it was time to say goodbye to our teachers. My English teacher Elena Aleksandrovna, my former maths teacher Alevtina Aleksandrovna, my former history teacher Galina Il'inichna and my literature teacher Alla Sergeevna each hugged me tightly. Like Russia, impatient to throw off the shackles of its Soviet past, I did not linger in my teachers' arms long enough. I felt grown up, almost restless to turn a new leaf. Just two days later I took a maths exam, got a "five" and a free place at the Ural State University of Economics. I was looking forward to a carefree summer, the freedom to read anything other than Tolstoy and go out with my friends. My parents, however, had something else in mind.

***

Earlier that year our school hosted a contest, which resembled a popular TV entertainment show, KVN. KVN is an abbreviation of *Klub Vesyelykh i Nakhodchivykh*, which means The Quick Fire Comedy Club. KVN originally appeared on Soviet television in 1961, and its popularity has not faded since. During the show a number of teams representing universities from all over Russia compete in a series of rounds, which include prepared sketches, impromptu questions and answers, a captains' round and a team song. Every performance is judged on originality and humour, and the contestants typically perform a parody of current affairs and popular culture. The show grew from student grassroots to become the incubator for Russia's show business and comedy talent.

We competed against two other schools which also specialised in English as a foreign language, and the entire contest was held in English. The judges included English teachers from the top universities in St. Petersburg and Moscow, including the revered MGIMO (Moscow State Institute of International Relations, possibly Russia's most prestigious academic institution). The head judge was Ian Worthington, a British diplomat who, a year later, opened the British Consulate in Ekaterinburg and became its first Consul General. I was the captain of our school team and we won. Our teachers, who sat in the assembly hall behind the judges, overheard the guests from Moscow saying that the "provincial students" spoke better English than the students from the capital. This remark was later repeated and retold so many times that if it were a rough stone it would have been polished into a perfectly smooth pebble by the many narrators. The head judge was impressed too. He shook my hand and asked me for my name. Worthington even shared the details of the contest with another expat, Dr. Falk Bomsdorf, head of the Friedrich Naumann Foundation (a German not-for-profit organisation, promoting democracy and liberal politics in Germany and worldwide) in Russia.

Dr. Bomsdorf was visiting from Moscow and meeting Ekaterinburg's government officials, academics and businessmen who worked with Germany. My father was one of them. They talked about commerce and current affairs, and then, quite unexpectedly, Dr. Bomsdorf asked about me and my father's plans for my education. He even asked to meet me. We had breakfast at the first modern B&B in Ekaterinburg, which advertised itself as a four-star hotel. Dr. Bomsdorf sported a thick moustache and rimless glasses. We talked about my school, my trip to London and my homestay in Germany. We spoke first in German then in English. My father had told me that Dr. Bomsdorf was looking to open an office for his foundation in Ekaterinburg and that perhaps one day I could work there, given my fluency in foreign languages. I was so preoccupied with exams that the memory of that meeting in early spring melted away as fast as the last of the winter snow.

"What if instead of getting a degree in Ekaterinburg, you could study in Germany – would you like that?" asked my father. He was driving us to the *dacha* just after we had found that I got into the Ural State University of Economics. It was a hot and sticky night and I was looking forward to a swim in the lake. I was wondering if Baba Lena had any *okroshka* left, craving the cold soup made with *kvas* which we always ate in the summer. My father's question startled me. I could see him grinning in the rear-view mirror. Mum, sitting next to him, turned to look at me, her eyes betraying a hint of anxiety.

It turned out that Dr. Bomsdorf knew the headmaster of one of Germany's most prestigious boarding schools, Schule Schloss Salem, situated in the south of Germany. He told my father about the school and even recommended me to the headmaster for a scholarship. My parents received an invitation to come to Salem for an interview, and the school offered to cover our travel expenses. My parents kept it secret from me until after I had taken all my exams.

"I would jump at it," I said without hesitation. I was sixteen. It took me just a second to decide to leave the safety of my parents' nest and embark on a foreign adventure.

***

Just two weeks later my parents and I were sitting in the office of the headmaster of Schule Schloss Salem, Dr. Bernhard Bueb. The room had a beautiful ornate ceiling and was decorated with dark wood, antique furniture and oil paintings. It was rather dark and smaller than I expected it to be, but like any headmaster's office, it appeared intimidating. Dr. Bueb himself was tall and lean with receding silver hair.

He wore a pale green blazer and light trousers. He looked more like a scholar than a headmaster. He greeted us warmly, then got straight down to business.

"Who did you vote for in the Russia's presidential elections?" he asked, leaning forward a little.

"My parents voted for Yeltsin, of course," I replied. "He stood for reforms. His main opponent from the Communist Party wants to isolate Russia from the West, re-nationalise industries and bring back state control."

Evidently, this was precisely what Dr. Bueb had hoped to hear. He smiled and the rest of the interview felt like a mere formality. I was enrolled to study for the International Baccalaureate (IB), a bilingual high-school programme with a diploma, accepted by universities worldwide. I was offered full scholarship and board. Later that morning I went to visit Schule Schloss Spetzgart, Salem's senior school which would be my home for the next two years. It was a castle standing on the top of the hill, overlooking Lake Constance, the spot where Germany, Austria and Switzerland meet. I was introduced to some students and one of the teachers, Frau Elvira Schäfer.

Frau Schäfer appeared young but her short hair was completely grey. She wore jeans and a neat but casual jumper, in stark contrast to my Russian teachers, who always dressed formally. She had been born in Russia to a German prisoner of war who had stayed in the Soviet Union. Following *perestroika*, Germany welcomed back its former citizens and their descendants, and Elvira Schäfer was one of many immigrants who had settled in Germany in the 1990s. Back in Russia she had taught German as a foreign language at university. In the new land she re-qualified to teach Russian instead. In Spetzgart, as part of the IB programme, she taught Russian as a native language, which was a literature course. I was her third ever student. Frau Schäfer had a nervous laugh which betrayed her lack of confidence.

"Tell me, Jana, who are your favourite authors?" she asked with a chuckle, pouring me a cup of coffee in her rooms at Spetzgart.

"I love Tolstoy and Bulgakov," I replied, "My favourite book is *The Master and Margarita*." I was pleased with the question.

Frau Schäfer nodded vigorously: "I remember reading Tolstoy's *War and Peace* at school," she mused, "it's *very* long, isn't it?"

I stared at her dumbfounded.

"*The Master and Margarita?* I could never finish that book," she continued.

Images of a severed head rolling by the Patriarshy Ponds, a demonic black cat walking on two legs and the naked Margarita, flying like a witch over Moscow by night, filled my mind, eager to spill out into the teacher's lifeless study. I clutched my cup so tightly, I feared it would break.

Oblivious to my inner turmoil, Frau Schäfer burst out laughing, stirring a lump of sugar in her coffee. I sat very still and felt a lump in my throat, which was refusing to melt.

Chapter VII in which I dyed my hair blue

After Yeltsin's re-election, Russia's oligarchs became invincible. They behaved as if they owned the country (which they did), controlling businesses and the media, influencing legislation and cajoling federal and local governors to do their bidding. Russians who voted for Yeltsin hoped that the government would build new institutions and infrastructure, support entrepreneurs and tackle crime. Instead, they got oligarchs greedily grabbing the state's remaining assets.

Meanwhile, Russian government forces struggled to defeat the rebels in Chechnya. It became a black hole, sucking in the State's money.

After the disbandment of the Soviet Union, Yeltsin failed to formulate a new vision for Russia or implement a consistent economic programme and address social concerns. It felt like Russia was a dirigible, tugged and swayed by impudent winds.

Ordinary people simply got on with their lives, just as they always had.

1996-1997, Schule Schloss Spetzgart, Germany

I shushed my alarm clock and reached to switch on the bedside light. The room was hot and the stench was unbearable. I could not quite work out whether Kowa was sleeping alone or whether her boyfriend was under the duvet with her. He was a big lad with long hair tied back in a ponytail, and his clothes and hair reeked of tobacco. I wondered if he ever showered. I hoped that my roommate Kowa would get bored of him soon so that I could sleep in peace without being woken in the night by their muffled humping. I got out of bed and picked up my toiletries, careful not to step on a used condom lying on the floor. The shower room was downstairs. I shut the door behind me with a bang.

Kowa was a fellow IB student from Chicago. She was slender and pretty, and made the most of the temporary freedom afforded her by a boarding school thousands of miles from home. Soon her parents would have to take her back to the States: the IB curriculum, developed in the 1960s in Switzerland, was so demanding that every year a couple of Spetzgart IB students failed their exams or dropped out before taking them. In my first term Kowa and I shared a room on the first floor of the school's main building. As an only child, I had never shared rooms before and I found it tricky. Once Kowa woke up with a nosebleed and yelled at me for setting the heating to the maximum temperature overnight. I grew up with central heating which was either "on" or "off" and had no idea it could be *adjusted*. I tolerated Kowa's nightly rendezvous for a while, but then I asked to switch roommates (and did), only to be shunned by her and her mates as a killjoy. My new roommate Nadine studied for Abitur (a set of exams taken at the end of high school in Germany) and usually got up an hour before the early breakfast to put on make-up and style her hair. She teased me for my cheap toiletries and high street clothes, but she was nice enough and let me use her hairdryer. Sometimes I joined her for the early breakfast at the school canteen, conveniently located in the same building, but often I went straight to class, like most students. Mid-morning, we all assembled at the canteen for the mandatory second breakfast, used as a forum for school announcements.

The canteen was a spacious room flooded with light from the ceiling-to-floor windows, which overlooked Lake Constance. It was the focal point of daily life at Schule Schloss Spetzgart. Breakfast was my favourite meal of the day. It was also a neat way to work out who was who at Spetzgart. The studious flocked to the early breakfast, which took place before the first two morning lessons. They spoke quietly, and the canteen resembled a funeral parlour with little light, the long faces of the still sleepy students and the methodical clunking of the spoons against cereal bowls. The canteen was transformed mid-morning when both teachers and students came in, filling the room with a resuscitating buzz. Freshly baked bread rolls were served with jam and honey, cheese and ham. My favourite rolls were made with rye flour mixed with linseeds and shaped like an upside-down ice tray. I would pull a warm cube apart, smother it with butter, top it with a dollop of honey and savour my roll, while observing the other students.

Beautiful and popular girls would pick at their rolls absent-mindedly and add a squeeze of orange to their tea. The girls of lower social status would have white bread rolls with sliced cheese and ham and add cream and sugar to their coffee. My roommate's friend Isabel was cursed with a bad case of acne and would soothe herself with two bread rolls topped with salami and an extra sprinkling of salt. The German girls on a scholarship often opted for pork pâté and frequently packed an extra roll in order to study in their rooms at lunchtime, skipping the formal meal. The IB students of the lowliest caste were fond of Nutella sandwiches. Many of them did not speak any German and needed comfort during a series of incomprehensible morning announcements.

The IB gang stuck out like a sore thumb among the hundred or so German Abitur students. It reminded me of a Russian salad *vinegret* with its strange ingredients like gherkins, cooked peas, carrots and beetroot thrown in together. There were three Poles who disliked me because of the Communism which had been inflicted on Eastern Europe by the Soviet Union. I was oblivious to their take on history and, like any Russian plucked straight from school history lessons, I thought that the Poles should be more grateful to us for defeating Hitler in the Second World War. There was a polite British boy and a punk Swiss girl who spoke eight languages but was not interested in studying. The heart and soul of the class was a Seychellois, who had been adopted by a German family for a few years to give her a European education. The girls lived together and broadly got on, save for the Poles who refused to play ball with the Russians and called us *kurvas* (sluts).

The IB programme at Spetzgart was a fairly recent venture. The official language of the course was English. Sadly, some of the Spetzgart's IB teachers did not speak it very well. Our advanced maths teacher, Herr Finkbeiner, whose surname joyously translated as "legs of a finch", liked to switch into German when he got particularly excited about the probability theory or calculus. I chose physics as my science and spent most lessons learning Polish. The teacher was an introvert who said little, whereas the Poles loved physics and the fact that I was clearly out of my depth. My father told me to take computer science and I dutifully attended the first couple of lessons, staring at the enormous textbook, listening to the soft-spoken teacher and getting poked by the Poles (whose parents worked as programmers). I approached the head of the IB programme and begged to switch to Art & Design, which was the only available alternative.

Back in Russia we studied drawing in junior school and then all arts disappeared from the school curriculum. Creative activities were meant to be pursued in one's spare time, and there were plenty of music, art and drama clubs around. At Spetzgart I found myself painting on a canvas for the very first time. It felt surreal to be messing around with paints and clay as part of an academic course. I half expected the teacher to round us up into a proper classroom and lecture us on the history of art, but he only kept uncovering new media to work with: clay, stone, steel, plaster and silk. The freedom of choice was unlike anything I had ever experienced in Russia. Over the next two years I experimented with jewellery design, calligraphy and printing under the gentle guidance of our teacher and surprised myself with the results. The IB exam required us to make an exhibition of our work, and I was allocated an airy room to display my sculptures, paintings and prints. I was certain that my works weren't particularly good but I hatched a plan to help me get noticed. Back in Ekaterinburg I once saw a body paint show by a local designer. I asked Juanita, a petite Spanish girl in the year below me, to be my model. I did not have any special paint so I used acrylics. Juanita was naked save for bikini briefs, and was patient while I transformed her into a nymph. The acrylic paint dried too quickly, creating webs of cracks, but the overall effect was stunning. I hid my nymph and let the examiner look at my other works first, with most of them themed to explore the sensuality and lives of women. Then I put on a Bryan Adam's song, *Have You Ever Really Loved a Woman,* and my muse walked into the centre of the room to the tunes of a Spanish guitar. Her curly hair dropped down to her shoulders and caught the sun streaming into the room. In her mouth she held a yellow daffodil to symbolise that a woman ought to love herself first and foremost. Was it cheesy? Most certainly. But it earned me a top mark in the Art & Design exam.

***

Schule Schloss Salem or Salem College, as it is now referred to in English, is considered one of the most elite boarding schools in Europe. It was founded in 1920 by Kurt Hahn, a German philosopher and an influential public figure who stood up to Adolf Hitler in the early 1930s and was forced to emigrate to Britain. He helped to found Gordonstoun in Scotland, Atlantic College in Wales and the Duke of Edinburgh Awards. Hahn's philosophy encompassed diversity and inclusion, collaboration and competition, empathy and caring. The school tried to honour these principles, but in truth, Salem was a tightly knit clique of young men and women who were remarkably alike. The majority of students came from wealthy, prominent and noble German families. Many inherited fine features from the selective genetic pool. While there was no uniform in high school, most students wore smart jeans, Ralph Lauren polo shirts and Barbour jackets. Before coming to Spetzgart for the last two years of school, most of them had already bonded in Hohenfels and Salem, the school's junior and main campuses.

The social life in Spetzgart revolved around a Club House, a shed built in the middle of the school grounds where the students gathered for dancing on Saturday nights. Every Saturday I diligently got ready and tried my luck at befriending the German elite. I clung on to every conversation like a drowning person to a log. I danced and smiled until my jaw ached from all the effort. My heart would stop if a popular boy danced with me for half a song. I'd go back to my room and piece the night together like a patchwork quilt, sewing in various bits of fabric, often with an imaginary thread. In hindsight, it was hopeless. I was an alien, too desperate to belong.

After a stint at the Club House, I'd go back to my building and often find Svetlana and Enikö, the Russian and Hungarian IB students from the year above, sitting on a couch in the hallway and playing Sheryl Crow, Tracy Chapman and Gloria Gaynor. The girls would be in their pyjamas, wearing no make-up and eating Nutella straight from a jar. They'd look at me knowingly and offer me a spoon.

Other Saturdays I would avoid the social melee altogether. After dinner I'd walk to Mädchenbau, one of the campus's buildings and knock on the door of Frau Schäfer. My Russian teacher and I got on well. I chose books I wanted to read and wrote essays on the topics I wanted to explore. I liked visiting her in the evenings because Frau Schäfer could be relied upon to have a tub of ice cream in her freezer. We were both partial toward walnut ice cream with a streak of maple syrup running through it. We'd talk a little, with the peals of her laughter irritating her otherwise quiet rooms.

***

Meanwhile, as far as I knew, all my former classmates had enrolled at one of the many institutions of higher education in Ekaterinburg. Masha got in to study architecture; Anya opted for a degree in government administration. Many of my fellow graduates chose to study economics. Polina, who was seriously gifted as an artist, was bullied by her mother to study "something useful to get a job in a bank". She did.

For young men, getting a place at university was especially important. Higher education shielded them from the army service. The Soviet war with Afghanistan (which had lasted for ten years until 1989) had returned many young lads home in sealed zinc coffins. Others remained haunted by post-traumatic stress for the rest of their lives. After the war, in the period of media openness, Afghanistan was dissected as a mistake. Its victims, army recruits who had volunteered or been sent there to help "the sacred international socialist cause" were considered unlucky and swiftly swept under the carpet of guilty national conscience. Still, Afghanistan became a lesson for all Russian mothers, who in the 1990s drummed it into their sons that compulsory military classes within the safety of university walls were infinitely preferable to the possibility of being sent to a war zone.

While I remained a schoolgirl, my classmates became university students, which meant they grew up quickly. Even if they still lived at home, they frequented university dorms, made new friends and appeared to shed all traces of childhood. At Russian universities, they had exams twice a year, which to them seemed less stressful than the more frequent tests we had endured at school. Our parents' generation took university exams *(sessiyi)* seriously: their results had determined how much funding students got from state universities. In the Soviet days, such monthly allowance was good enough to get by. At the end of 1990s, a student with good marks received 120 roubles, while a student with top marks received 180 roubles a month. That was just about enough to buy a Maybelline lipstick. When I came back to Ekaterinburg during school holidays, I met up with some friends at Mac Peak, Ekaterinburg's first fast food restaurant, which was a desperate imitation of MacDonald's and a popular meeting point for status-craving youths. An order of a burger and fries (which were home-cooked and therefore actually tasty) would set a student back half a monthly stipend. Many students got part-time jobs, which were relatively easy to find, thanks to the growing economy. When I told my friends about my boarding school woes, my concerns appeared childish in the context of their new, more adult lives.

***

Back in Germany, I often kept my own company on weekends. Sometimes I would catch a bus to a nearby town. Überlingen is a small resort town on Lake Constance with a dainty promenade and expensive cafés frequented by wealthy retirees and tourists. In May the restaurants would serve soused young herring with boiled new potatoes, fresh dill and sliced onion, a German speciality called *Matjes*. Then the *Spargel* (asparagus) season would arrive, and Germans from all over Baden-Württemberg would descend on the sunny terraces of Überlingen to devour perfectly straight spears of white asparagus with silky hollandaise sauce. All year round the local cafés offered *Kaffee und Kuchen* (coffee and cake), and I would cruise around, admiring apple strudel, plum crumble and *Schwarzwaldkuchen* (Black Forest Gateau) through the display windows. At Christmas time I would treat myself to a slice of *Mohnstollen*, a rolled cake filled with marzipan and poppy seeds and covered with icing sugar, like a babe wrapped in a blanket.

It was sometime after the Christmas break of my first year at Spetzgart that I decided to dye my hair blue. Perhaps I was inspired by my classmate Francesca, who came back from the holidays with subtle red highlights in her brown hair. I got hold of some dye from a party shop in Überlingen and covered my long, bleached blond hair with thick blue paint. The effect was striking – until I washed my hair a couple of days later. The dye disappeared down the bathroom drain, leaving my hair a streaky palette of various shades of green. I was at boarding school with no place to hide. I still had to attend classes, basketball practice and school meals, pretending to be nonchalant. The Poles had a field day. My roommate Nadine said *selbst schuld* (own fault), as she carefully pressed an oil-absorbing tissue to her nose, then powdered it again.

That week the Club House was out of the question, and I found myself in the library. It was the only place guaranteed to be empty on a Saturday night. I walked in and was heading for a solitary desk in the corner when I bumped into my economics teacher, Herr Niedinger. Anton Niedinger was a lanky South African with a bowl haircut and round glasses. He was in his thirties and appeared a little quirky, usually wearing a knitted cardigan and walking around the campus with *The Economist* and a weekly horoscope tucked under his arm. He was, however, one of those teachers who genuinely wanted his students to do well in life. In addition to teaching, he was also one of the school's career counsellors.

"Jana! What are you doing in the library on a Saturday night?" said Herr Niedinger, emphasising the "t" in his South African accent.

"Hiding my mermaid hair," I said with a sigh. There was little point in making up false excuses. "And you?"

"I'm working on a school newsletter. Have you heard that Alex Krings got into Oxford? That's where *you* should be applying to next year."

Alex Krings was a year above me and was studying for the German Abitur. He went on to Oxford to study Law. It was not Alex, though, who caught my attention, but Oxford. I had no plans beyond the IB, and it was hugely flattering to hear my economics teacher suggest that I should apply to such a famous university.

"I'd like to study economics," I said, surprising myself.

Economics had quickly become my favourite subject at Spetzgart. It was so different from anything I'd come across in Russia. I was fascinated by the laws of supply and demand, determining prices in free markets, and by how firms make their business decisions. In the Soviet Union prices and output were set by the State, which was also responsible for allocating all resources. Unemployment was unheard of before *perestroika*. The exchange rates were artificially fixed. It was stupefying to realise the scale of planning the Soviet statisticians had been undertaking and the complexity of the work involved. It was also surprising to me, after just a few months of economics lessons, that the Soviet Union had lasted for as long as it did. Herr Niedinger was not an economist by training; he taught English literature as well, but he was a good teacher, genuinely interested in the subject himself.

"Have a look here," said Herr Niedinger, handing me a British university catalogue. Flicking through it, I noticed that it already had bookmarks for Oxford, Cambridge and the London School of Economics.

I left the library to return to my room. The school buildings were enveloped in darkness and I could hear the music coming from the Club House. The gravel crunched under my feet, and I briefly imagined it was snow. The night sky was clear and here, away from the competing city lights, the stars came out unabashedly. I settled in bed with my own copy of the *Oxford Advanced Learner's Dictionary*. I traced the word "OXFORD" with my finger, then flicked through the delicate pages. I fell asleep with the Oxford dictionary on my lap.

Chapter VIII in which the bubble burst

After Yeltsin was re-elected, foreign investment poured into Russia. The government was financing its spending by issuing short-term bonds with increasingly high yields. Both local and foreign speculators, especially those who got burned in Asia and were looking for new opportunities in the emerging markets, piled their money into Russia. Moscow became a magnet for financial investors, who were buying up Russia's government bonds by day and partying at its clubs by night. No one noticed that Moscow and other big cities were but Potemkin villages, propped up to impress and mask the staggering economy, wage arrears and poverty.

By 1998, a costly war in Chechnya and unsustainable social spending took their toll on the Russian state coffers. In addition, the government was spending its foreign currency reserves to support the rouble pegged to the US dollar (at six roubles to a dollar). The US dollar became Russia's unofficial currency: many entrepreneurs took out loans in US dollars to grow their companies. Virtually all private businesses used US dollars to price their goods and services.

London and Oxford, December 1997

They were pouring out of Victoria station: girls in skimpy outfits with their bare legs covered in goosebumps, unsteady in summer stilettos. Boys too followed in packs, drenched in cheap aftershave and jittery with testosterone. Hours later they returned, swaying a little, swearing a lot, loud and happy after a night out in London. From my vantage point, sitting on the floor just outside the station, I could watch them unabashedly without intrusion. A person sleeping on the street in London is practically invisible. I wore a long winter coat, a thick scarf and gloves, but just looking at the scantily dressed English made me shiver. I pulled my knees tighter towards me and urged the long December night to pass quickly.

About a month earlier I had received a letter from Oxford inviting me for an interview. I applied to study Economics & Management and hoped that my open application – I didn't apply to any particular college – would raise my chances of getting in. The invitation for an interview arrived from St. Catherine's College, with Balliol listed as a second choice. Frau Spach, the chain-smoking headmaster's secretary, hugged me, drew deeply on her cigarette and allowed me to make an international call from her telephone. I phoned my parents and asked for an early present for my eighteenth birthday: a plane ticket to London. They obliged and I hugged Frau Spach again, giddy with smoke and my good fortune.

My father paid for my trip and suggested that I stay in London for a couple of days before travelling to Oxford. I arrived at Victoria and found the hotel my father had booked for me. Unfortunately, the reception staff knew nothing about my reservation. "Don't worry, we've got some availability," they said and quoted me a rate which made my heart sink. I had changed my money earlier and figured out that one night at a hotel would wipe half of my budget for the entire trip. I turned around and walked back to the station, resolving to stay up all night. It was already dark and very cold. I found a McDonald's, a cheap but not convincingly cheerful retreat, with other customers looking lonely and miserable. As night fell I settled down by the entrance to the station for my vigil, hoping I wouldn't get into trouble with the police. I crumpled the McDonald's cup as soon as I finished my tea so that no one would get the wrong idea.

The next morning, I found a cheap B&B and dropped my luggage in a poky room before running out to explore London. Just as catching up with an old friend feels warm and effortless, so my reunion with London put me at ease and filled me with confidence. I walked around all day, taking in familiar sights and feeling childishly superior to other tourists, who were discovering London for the first time. The next day I travelled to Oxford and presented myself at the Porters' Lodge (or reception) of St. Catherine's College. Oxford's newest college, it was founded in 1962 and built by a Danish architect, Arne Jacobsen. Some refer to Jacobsen's visionary achievement as a modern masterpiece. The sombre style of his buildings in a traditional quadrangle layout grew on me over the years, but when I first saw St. Catherine's on that December afternoon in 1997, it looked like an ugly duckling among the swans. The library and the residence halls appeared dark and austere, so unlike the magnificent buildings of the ancient colleges I had passed on the way from the station. St. Catherine's just looked too *modern*. Worse, I was greeted by a scruffy youth wearing a maroon hoodie and old trainers, who introduced himself as Doron, an interview coordinator. Apparently, he was an Oxford student! "All right?" asked Doron. I felt like a tourist disappointed by the absence of fog in London.

At St. Catherine's I had two interviews with Economics

and Management tutors. Like every other candidate, I also had to take an Oxford entrance exam. My confidence evaporated as soon as I opened the paper. Some of the questions were intended to test my command of English and appeared to be mocking me. They synched with the voice in my head shouting: "An impostor! She squatted at Victoria and now she wants to get into Oxford! Hahaha." The task was to define some words and then use them in sentences. One word was "to enervate" and another was "capricious". I was drained trying to figure out what the former meant and made some erratic attempts to use the latter. I was crestfallen and rushed out of the exam room. Doron, who was wearing the same horrible hoodie as the day before, offered me a cup of tepid tea as a consolation and walked me to my Economics interview.

I was greeted by a young man with a nest of unkempt hair, wearing black jeans and a black t-shirt, who introduced himself as "David". I nearly asked him for the whereabouts of Dr. David Myatt, then the penny dropped. He asked "How is it going?" and I began telling him about my disastrous performance in the written test. David promptly steered me away from a "boring paper no one cares about" to economics, Prisoner's Dilemma (the most common game taught as an introduction to game theory) and the Simpsons (David's favourite TV series, frequently doubling as a setting for modelling economic behaviour). The conversation was so informal, we might have been chatting in a pub. An Oxford don, I later realised, is much like a sensible employer, looking to hire a person he would actually enjoy working with.

***

I got an offer from St. Catherine's College, conditional upon my IB results. I sat the exams and said good-bye to Salem. At the time, I felt a little tearful. In truth, I probably cried over my failure to fit in. I felt like an outsider not because I was Russian, but because I didn't belong to the fabulously rich German elite. As soon as I returned to Russia, I felt happier in the buzz and anonymity of a big city after being confined to the walls of a boarding school. It was the summer of 1998 and I found myself in a city I barely recognised. Ekaterinburg resembled a department store still bearing the same name but with a brand new collection on show. I took a trolley-bus into the city centre and marvelled at the smart outdoor advertising, glossy new shopping centres and sleek office buildings. I noticed there were many new banks with similar names and logos. The streets were congested with *inomarki* (foreign-made cars), including the odd Jaguar or Porsche. The ubiquitous kiosks selling snacks had largely disappeared, but retail stores had mushroomed. Many new shops occupied former ground-floor flats, which the previous owners had sold to commercial developers. In Baba Tonya's block of flats, a lingerie store had opened, providing plenty for the elderly residents to gossip about. Only my babushka's kitchen looked and smelled exactly as I remembered it: of the bay leaves with which she always used to flavour the water when cooking *pelmeni* (traditional Russian dumplings). Babushka appeared frailer but happy to have me back for the summer.

Ekaterinburg had undergone a complete makeover thanks to local and foreign investment. Homegrown businessmen donated money to restore old churches, which were now adorned with gold, just like their benefactors. Foreign investors too rushed to grab the spoils of the wild East. Ford and Toyota had opened dealerships to sell their cars to a new breed of Russians: the middle class. Global retail, pharmaceutical and electronics brands opened offices in Ekaterinburg and were busy recruiting top talent. They paid in "*u.e.*", which was an abbreviation for "nominal units" – the official name for US dollars, the unofficial currency of Russia at the end of the 1990s. Prices in designer shops were in *u.e.*, salaries were discussed in *u.e.* and a trip to Spain on a direct charter flight from Ekaterinburg, previously an extravagant dream, became a reality, subject to possessing a wad of *u.e.* Anya and Masha showed me around the city's new social establishments. There was a Scottish pub called Gordon's, situated behind the Theatre of Opera and Ballet, and a German-style watering hole called Dynamo right by the university. Both bars resembled their Western ancestors only in their design and the whisky and beer on the menu. Their glamorous clientele consisted of the local rich list and foreign expats who worked for the British and German consulates, Lufthansa and Coca Cola. The bars served tomatoes with imported mozzarella and had a price list in *u.e.*, but one *obviously* had to pay for everything in roubles. My friends thought I'd be delighted, but I mostly preferred *Olivier* salad and *rassol'nik* (a classic Russian soup with pearl barley, pickled cucumbers and brine).

Masha was working as a part-time interior designer at her mother's architecture firm. Anya, who was studying government administration and was interested in politics, joined her father at Transformation of Urals *(Preobrazheniye Urala)*, one of several local political parties represented in the legislative assembly of the Sverdlovsk *oblast* (federal district, which retained the name "Sverdlovsk" even though the city itself was renamed Ekaterinburg). Back then the assembly had significant regional powers; in 2011 Vladimir Putin would restore most of Moscow's control.

Once Anya got some work experience, she set up her own political PR firm and ran it for a couple of years. Our parents, who had done well in the *perestroika* era, had passed entrepreneurial instincts on to us. While they definitely helped us with their business connections, we were eager to make our own paths.

My father helped me get a summer job as an assistant to the general manager of the Atrium Palace Hotel, a grand business hotel which was built in the centre of Ekaterinburg by a group of Ural investors, who had made their money in the privatised non-ferrous metals and energy industries. It was a grand business hotel, aspiring to earn five stars, and designed by Western standards. The investors hired a seasoned Austrian general manager, Hansjörg Stohs, a trim man in his sixties, a tireless workaholic who enjoyed the challenge of opening hotels in Russia. The management team also included other specialists from Austria, Britain, Argentina and Moscow. The expats and the top Ekaterinburg talent were all crammed together in a large office on the top floor of the hotel, while the rest of the floors were still being built and furnished. In the two months ahead of the opening, I translated the menus and helped the British chefs interview their staff, I shadowed the sales and marketing manager as she was preparing for the launch and ran around the site with Hansjörg Stohs, inspecting rooms, commercial refrigerators, arguing with the owners, sampling cake for the downstairs Viennese café and shouting at the builders who installed the toilet roll holders out of reach. The Atrium Palace Hotel was the talk of the town, and I was spending all my time there, noticing little else, keen as mustard.

I found out that I got into Oxford one night after work.

I was home alone. My parents usually drove to the *dacha* in the evenings to escape from the heat of the city. The call came from our IB coordinator, a teacher I had never really got to know, who delivered what was then the happiest news of my life to date. Her tone was as matter-of-fact as a dentist congratulating me on the healthy state of my teeth after a routine check-up. I didn't care though.

I wanted to share my news with the whole world: "I am going to Oxford!" Instead I called Baba Tonya.

"You'll be leaving again", she said with resignation, adding "One day you'll become an *inostranka* (a foreigner)."

That summer I believed that everything was possible, that doors would always open for me, that the future was full of enticing possibilities and that I would make the most of them all.

And then the rouble crashed.

On 17th August 1998, the Russian government defaulted on its foreign and domestic debt. In the months leading up to default, the government kept issuing new high-yield bonds to repay the maturing ones. In June 1998, the newly appointed Prime Minister Sergey Kiriyenko (who was just thirty-five years old at the time) ratcheted up the interest on Russia's bonds to 150%. At that point investors finally smelled a rat and were desperate to get out. The IMF and the World Bank came to the government's help with a US$22 billion package to inject money into the economy and counterbalance the capital outflow, but it was too late. The Russian stock market plummeted. The government eased its support for the rouble and then abandoned it altogether, which led to its rapid devaluation relative to the US dollar and other currencies. Russia declared a moratorium on foreign debt payments, which meant that many Western investors lost their money, while some Russian banks, possibly those with better connections, were saved from having to close down.

While the economic history books can now expertly piece together the chain of events that led to the crisis and explain its inevitability, the situation in Russia at the end of August 1998 was akin to the proverbial car crash. People who went to their *dachas* on weekends, made daily *u.e.* calculations in their heads and hoped to go to Spain on holiday did not see it coming. These people stormed the banks in an attempt to withdraw their savings from the banks, but were blocked by security guards. Some of the victims of the crash were small businessmen who had taken out loans denominated in *u.e.* when one US dollar cost six roubles. Within a month, the exchange rate of the free-floating Russian currency was twenty-one roubles for a dollar. My father had taken out a loan to purchase retail stock in Germany. There were no longer any customers to buy his products at tripled prices, only trade creditors and bankers wanting payment. His business was wiped out, and he nearly went bankrupt.

The British consulate refused my application for a student

visa on the grounds that they feared we would not have enough money to pay my tuition fees. In hindsight, it was a perfectly rational, impersonal decision. But that wasn't how I saw it at the time. The face of the pale woman with mousy hair who had delivered the verdict to me across the window separating the beggars from those deciding their fortunes is forever imprinted in my mind as a symbol of gross injustice. Like any Russian, I did not blame the authority itself, but its messenger. I was in despair; my future, already neatly packed into a suitcase, had been lost, like misplaced luggage.

"Higher education is pointless," declared my boss after our usual inspection of the hotel first thing in the morning. We were sitting at the breakfast table inside the stunning atrium of the quiet hotel, which had been opened in the middle of the crisis and now faced hard times. Hansjörg Stohs popped a warm miniature Danish pastry into his mouth and continued, "Your parents have to pay for your degree, then you'll get married, have children and say good-bye to your career aspirations. Save yourself the time and money. Get a job – you don't need a piece of paper for that." He drained his coffee cup and sat back in his chair. Hansjörg Stohs was a wise man, but he had not got an offer from Oxford. I wrote to St. Catherine's College and asked to defer my admission by a year. Fortunately, the College agreed.

***

My grandfather died on 2nd April 1999, five days before his seventy-fifth birthday. His former history department had been planning a big celebration, with many former students expected to come to Ekaterinburg from all over Russia and the former Soviet republics. He too was looking forward to the big day because, like any intellectual, he loved a good dinner conversation. On 2nd April, the spring took its first decisive step of that year, maddening the sparrows and softening the previous year's snow. My grandfather headed over to his garage, took out a cast iron pole and began breaking the ice, impatient to open the gates and take his car to the *dacha*. He was found lying in front of the garage with the heavy pole beside him. *Dedushka* had suffered a heart attack (his fourth). He should have known better than to undertake something so strenuous. He knew, of course, that he would have been better off staying put and waiting for spring to melt the ice naturally, but sitting still was alien to him. Before he died he had written two and a half volumes of *The History of Soviet Totalitarianism,* examining the human cost of Soviet industrialisation, a subject which had scarcely been discussed before. He still looked after the *dacha*, went hunting, fishing and mushroom picking. He worked and lived like he meant it. At his funeral people recalled his strong will, his rich intellect and his restless passion for life.

***

In September 1999, the pale, mousy-haired woman at the British consulate issued me a visa to travel to the UK. I was triumphant, as if it was my personal victory, rather than growing confidence in the Russian economy, supported by the rising oil prices. I spent a few months working for my father, studying at the Ural State University of Economics for a semester and doing a work placement at the Ekaterinburg branch of German airline Lufthansa. It all seemed transitory, not challenging enough, small change in comparison to my real aspirations. A new sticker in my passport was one matter, but tuition fees presented another problem. My father's business, dependent on imports, had suffered a heavy blow. He struggled to pay salaries and keep his firm afloat. He had to ask friends to help us pay for my tuition and accommodation at Oxford. They lent us enough to cover the first term. I was on my way.

Chapter IX in which two men of mystery appeared: Putin and Pugh

After Russia's financial crisis in August 1998, Yeltsin appointed 69-year-old Evgeny Primakov as his new prime minister. Primakov was a steady hand. His appointment was intended to settle the nation. As a dinosaur of the Soviet era, he was also meant to appease the communists, who dominated the Duma.

Primakov largely left the economy to its own devices. He operated via the old network, relying on security services and the apparatchiks, soon consolidating power and support from 'red' anti-market and anti-liberal factions, displeasing the journalists, the oligarchs and Yeltsin himself. Perhaps Yeltsin did not like the prime minister's rising popularity or maybe his backers began to worry about losing their influence, especially after some of their firms had been raided by the tax police. In his memoirs, Yeltsin wrote that "Primakov's continued presence in power threatened to polarise society" and sacked him.

"The general public is increasingly looking for a new attribute in the State," wrote Yeltsin, "a steel kernel of sorts, which will strengthen the frame of political power. We need a man who is intelligent and cultured, democratic, who thinks anew, but who is firm, in a military way."

The 'chosen one' was Vladimir Putin, an alumnus of the FSB (Federal Security Service, formerly the KGB) and St. Petersburg's administration. In August 1999 Yeltsin appointed Putin as prime minister and named him his successor.

October – December 1999, Oxford

As a boisterous crowd of students poured from the narrow Holywell Street out into Broad Street, many came to an abrupt halt. It was impossible not to stare at the sheer beauty of the sights we beheld. The Bodleian Library buildings and the Sheldonian Theatre, a ceremonial hall designed by Sir Christopher Wren, stood right in front of us and yet these buildings, which appear on every Oxford brochure, seemed surreal. The capricious British weather had settled on a glorious day for our matriculation, a formal ceremony of being enrolled at university, which took place at the Sheldonian on the first Saturday of October. I stopped to take it all in, squinting into the sun. Like everyone else, I was wearing *sub fusc* (from the Latin *sub fuscus,* meaning dark brown): a ceremonial outfit including black and white formal clothes, a black gown, a tie or a ribbon and a mortar board, traditionally worn by Oxford students for matriculation and exams.

The gown, mortar board and velvet ribbon I had bought for the ceremony had nearly wiped out all the cash my parents had given me. A microeconomics textbook I got from Blackwell's on Broad Street finished the job. Blackwell's, a quaint bookshop with a small entrance opening into a cavernous wonderland, was my favourite place in Oxford. It had an intoxicating smell emanating from shelf upon shelf of brand new books. Upstairs there was a café where customers could flick through the pages of small treasures while having a cup of coffee. I could afford neither novels nor coffee but I popped into the bookshop every single time I walked past it, tracing the precious spines with my fingers and reading handwritten recommendation cards. I was pleased to see Bulgakov's *The Master and Margarita* in four different translations with imaginatively designed paperback covers. In Soviet days we had only had hardbacks; in the 1990s pulp fiction flooded Russian stores with stories of gruesome crime and cheap romance. It was not until the literary translator Grigory Chkhartishvili, writing under the pen name Boris Akunin, came up with historic mysteries featuring the captivating detective Erast Fandorin that the Russians got something new they could read in public without wrapping embarrassing paperbacks in old newspapers. After drooling over books, I would leave Blackwell's with *toska*, a feeling of longing or sadness, once described by the Russian émigré writer Vladimir Nabokov as a word with no English equivalent. He defined *toska* as "a dull ache of the soul".

The Monday after matriculation I had my first microeconomics lecture at the Exam Schools, just down the road from Catz, as we called St. Catherine's College. My classmate Jess suggested we "grab a sandwich" on the way back to College. For a moment, I thought she was suggesting we run off with a sandwich without paying – but then I saw her stiletto shoes and dismissed the idea. She ordered a chicken, avocado and bacon baguette. I looked up at the chalk board with prices and mumbled that I wasn't hungry just yet. We walked up Longwall Street towards Catz. It was clear to me I had to find a job and fast.

Back at Catz I went for lunch in the College Hall, designed by the reliably austere Arne Jacobsen and decorated with gargantuan tapestries made by a former Catz student. I approached the self-service table gingerly, having had an unsavoury incident earlier in the day. In the morning, I had joined the queue of larks (as we refer to early risers in Russian) and got some toast for breakfast. There was a bowl with a selection of butter, margarine and jam. I hoped they might have honey, because I only liked the homemade jams my grandmothers made. I found something which looked like dark honey with an unusual label on top. A fellow fresher sitting opposite me at the long breakfast table did warn me to spread it thinly, but I layered this mysterious "marmite" generously over my buttered toast and took a large bite. I regretted it.

For lunch I picked a large baked potato, which at only ninety pence seemed good value, and sat opposite another classmate, Matt. Matt, who was from Reading, later acquired the nickname "Hairy Matt" because although he would shave every morning, he'd still sprout stubble by the end of the evening. On his plate he had half a baguette, which he had sliced horizontally, buttered and filled with chips! Like everyone else on the planet, I thought the English only ate fish, chips and mushy peas but here they were stretching the palate to new culinary heights. In addition to marmite on toast and chips baguette, I discovered pickled eggs, the national obsession with tinned tuna and a cereal called Weetabix, which, once soaked in milk, unless eaten at once resembled a roll of toilet paper dropped into the loo. Chips were revered and eaten with gravy, dipped in curry sauce or covered in hot baked beans and grated cheese. The latter somehow became my favourite late night snack, sold by the legendary Hassan from his white kebab van, which appeared on Broad Street at night, like a beacon helping to guide the unsteady vessels in the dark.

The following day we had our first management lecture,

held in temporary quarters of the Saïd Business School on George Street. The Oxford undergraduate management faculty and the graduate business school were founded in 1996 and named after its main benefactor, Wafic Saïd, a Saudi-Syrian billionaire, who allegedly made his money facilitating the Al-Yamamah arms deal between the United Kingdom and Saudi Arabia in the 1980s. If there was a suspicion that our education was being paid for by funding the war in the Middle East, I did not ask any questions. I just felt lucky to be in Oxford. After the lecture I strolled along Cornmarket, a cobbled pedestrian street in the centre of the city, looking for something to eat (as ever). Briefly distracted by the smell of expensive, freshly made espresso coffee from an open-air stall by the church, I walked into a Co-op, a small budget supermarket which was later closed down, unable to justify the premium rent. There I examined each shelf with forensic curiosity, finally laying my eyes on the bright orange packets of Ginger Nuts. I had never tasted ginger before, but it was the price tag that I found irresistible: 32p. I bought three packs and subsisted on them for the next three days.

My British food education continued as I got a job as a waitress at the Catz Formal Hall that same week. Every weeknight, dinner was served in College with the dons wearing black robes and sitting at the so-called High Table, which stood on a raised platform at the head of the hall. The dons enjoyed *haute cuisine* and used cutlery that was also designed by the prolific Arne Jacobsen. Unlike his larger works, the cutlery was exquisite, which is why it was regularly pinched and had to be re-ordered. The students weren't required to dress formally and their food was subsidised. A three-course meal cost less than three pounds and was served by student waiters, like me, who were paid eight pounds an hour and received a free meal after work. Once I got the hang of it, I moved up in the world and often served at the High Table where the pay was even better and I could eavesdrop on the dons' conversations. And so I began dishing out potted gammon, toad in the hole and spotted dick to students, and more refined foods to the dons, five nights a week. On Saturdays I sometimes picked up additional work in private dining rooms or earned a tenner as a cashier charging students for their cheap and cheerful defrosted and deep-fried chicken kievs, which sadly bore no resemblance to the juicy cutlets of the finest Soviet dining establishments.

Learning the ropes of waitressing was easy; studying in Oxford was not. For economics, we had to attend lectures, which were mostly uninspiring, read by academics who detested having to leave their research lairs. Every week we had to tackle a problem, which was discussed in a small group seminar (there were just five of us in my Economics & Management class at Catz). For this we had to read academic papers and textbooks, which, unlike school economics books, were brimming with formulas. The academic papers were so complicated that I never tried to read them beyond their abstracts. For Management tutorials, which were held in line with Oxford tradition with just two students and a tutor, each week we had to write an essay, which was then marked with Greek letter grades, with Alpha being the top mark. But first we had to hunt down academic articles recommended for our essay assignments. Some were available online, but access wasn't free. Most were stored in the Oxford libraries. I would turn up at the Bodleian with my English-Russian dictionary and sit down to read a paper and take notes. Pretty quickly, I realised that I simply did not have time to check every single new word in my dictionary, not least because running around Oxford (I could not afford to buy a bike just yet) with an extra volume was a nuisance.

"Hey, have you read *Puff* yet?" I once asked Jess, as I bumped into her leaving the library. I was hunting down an important paper on organisational design, marked on our assignment sheet in **bold**.

"Hi darling, I haven't… Was he on the list? I don't recall…" said Jess.

"He was! I'm sure – look!" I dug out my assignment sheet.

"Oh, you mean *Pew!*" said Jess, laughing and pointing to a paper by *Derek Pugh et al.*

Finally, after all the running around, reading, taking notes and writing, I'd submit my essay and go to a tutorial the next day. Our Management tutor, Alison Thomas, was a thin woman with short slate-coloured hair and deeply penetrating eyes. She did not suffer fools gladly. Alison had a habit of pursing her lips sideways, a subtle gesture which implied anything from "Hmmm" to "You are a moron". At the beginning, it seemed to me she was doing it every time I opened my mouth, so I let my classmate Tim do the talking. That was a mistake. Tim was from Belfast and I could not understand a word he was saying. For example, it took me a while to realise that his name was actually "Tim" and not "Tam" as he had introduced himself. During our first management tutorial together, I was astonished to see Alison nodding and asking him encouraging questions to elaborate on his view – to me, he was talking gibberish. What followed was even more appalling: I got a Beta for my essay.

Many young bright people come to Oxford expecting to enlighten the world with their brilliance. They quickly realise that their playing field has changed from a random but fair selection of school students to an exceptionally high concentration of both ability and ambition. On the surface, Oxford students may go out drinking several nights a week and rather be seen dead than in a library, but deep down they are often nurtured overachievers with a wildly competitive streak. When Tim, the incomprehensible Northern Irishman, got a higher mark for his essay than I did, I jolted like a racehorse at the sound of a start gun. I was determined to score an Alpha, get the hang of economic equations and management theories and not fall behind. It did not occur to me then, but I belonged to a breed of people who looked at a life as a running track, always searching for a new challenge to spur them on.

Looking back, my first term at Oxford was a blur of studying hard, waiting on tables and trying to fit in. Naturally, it involved going to student nights at Oxford clubs with drinks for a pound each and occasional all-you-can-drink parties with cheap vodka, vaguely diluted with juice or whatever was the content of the white supermarket cartons with blue stripes and the red promise of "value". I did not join any clubs or societies and could scarcely believe that some people found time for drama or sport. My classmate Matthew took up rowing. He and his fellow lunatics would get up at the crack of dawn and cycle to the river Isis in the south of Oxford for a morning outing. On inclement November mornings Matthew would be spotted returning to College, wearing lycra and covered in mud. None of it appealed to me. From my bedroom window, overlooking the Catz quad, I would see rowers, students who had gotten lucky the night before and the less lucky ones with early morning lectures. I'd boil water for a cup of instant coffee, steal a dash of milk from the communal fridge and pore over a textbook. Before I knew it, Michaelmas, the first term in the Oxford calendar, was over.

The students departed, eager to go back to their family nests for a spell of home-cooked meals and maternal pampering. I stayed in College for a couple of weeks in December to work as a waitress during the busy conference season. Outside term times, St. Catherine's was a money-making machine offering catering and accommodation to academic and corporate clients. In the morning we would meet in Hall to polish glasses and silver and lay the tables for lunch. After lunch service and cleaning up we had a break until dinner. I remember running to Blackwell's and buying *Harry Potter and the Philosopher's Stone* in anticipation of my earnings from the conference season. I'd then climb into my bed and read the book voraciously, enjoying a much-needed break from *Pugh et al.* Back in Hall, we'd be bossed around by Linda, an unpleasant conference manager. She was a local resident, a "town" woman. The power she held over "gown", the Oxford students, was nectar to her. I consoled myself after work with chocolate and mince pies.

Sometimes a few of us would go to the pub. I remember talking to a history student interested in twentieth-century Russia. He asked me about my recollection of the Cold War years before the Berlin Wall had been taken down.

"I really don't remember us ever talking about it. I'd not even heard the term "Cold War" until I came to the UK," I said.

"Seriously?"

"I mean we had gas mask training at primary school and there were reports of new missiles being developed to catch the Americans, but it was all in the spirit of competition, you know, along with the space race and the Olympics. I don't think I'd be here now if I had been brought up on the war rhetoric."

"I reckon you're a Russian spy, pulling my leg."

"Makes a change from being called a daughter of an oligarch!"

***

One night after the service I discovered a thick envelope in my pigeon hole with my father's writing on it. I ripped it open on the way back to my room, nearly colliding with Doron, who was in his final year at Catz, and was once again meeting and greeting new hopefuls. Now I too was wearing a casual hoodie on top of my white waitressing shirt. In the envelope I found a birthday card from my parents and two letters: one from Baba Tonya and one from my father. I rushed to my room, drew the thick curtains, turned on my bedside lamp and climbed under the duvet. I glanced through the birthday card and put it on a shelf above the bed. Its Russian design seemed so alien juxtaposed with the English-language textbooks behind it.

My father had written me a long letter with details of his

aspirations for me. His instructions covered every aspect of my life: studies, work, future career and even love. He was proud of me but he wanted me to go further and perhaps realise his own dreams. By the end of page four, he finally got to the point: he was struggling to make ends meet. I wasn't taken by surprise. He had first written to me about my tuition fees back in October, just after I had started my first term. Now my father had sold a Russian Orthodox icon he had bought with some of the first money he'd ever made, and borrowed more from his friends. He had just managed to scrape together enough money to pay for the remainder of my first year at Oxford. That was a relief.

"As for the next academic year, I've run out of ideas," he wrote. I knew he'd do anything for me, yet now he was asking me to help myself.

"Yana, you have three options," he wrote, adding that he liked the last one best. "Try to get a job over the summer with a company which will agree to cover your tuition." I sighed. I already knew that big companies only wanted second-year students, and corporate sponsorships were extremely rare. I continued reading: "Find a British husband, so that you don't have to pay overseas fees." I sighed again. The third option was: "Come back to Russia." With that I opened the second letter from my increasingly frail Baba Tonya, who was eighty-five at the time.

She asked me about my life *there*. She said she was glad I liked it *there* and wished me to be happy. She worried I was working too hard. She wrote about feeling too weak to go out. She said she was losing her sight, and her words danced on the page, as if to illustrate it. "Imagine how hard it is to be alone all the time," she wrote. Tears began streaming down my face. I knew exactly how she felt. It was bad enough to strive to make a living far away from home, but now the fragile possibilities of my future were about to be shattered again, and I had no one to turn to for help.

Chapter X in which I fell down a rabbit hole

On 31st December 1999, Boris Yeltsin resigned as Russia's president, taking the country and the rest of the world by surprise. In his speech, broadcast on that momentous New Year's Eve, he asked Russians to forgive him for unrealised dreams and crushed hopes. "It turned out that it was impossible to jump from the grey, stagnant, totalitarian past straight into the bright, abundant and civilised future."

Yeltsin announced that prime minister Putin would act as president until the elections scheduled for March 2000.

Anointed by Yeltsin, Putin represented continuity of power. Since becoming prime minister in August 1999, he had proven himself to be firm and decisive. When Chechen warlords entered the Russian republic of Dagestan, Putin (with Yeltsin's blessing) ordered Russian troops to retaliate. When explosives were detonated in four residential blocks of flats in Moscow, Buynaksk and Volgodonsk, Putin vowed to avenge the innocent victims and track down the Chechen terrorists, who had been reported as culprits. His approval ratings shot up.

Physically, the contrast between the outgoing and the new leader could not have been more stark. Addressing the nation on the eve of the new millennium, Yeltsin looked old and ashen. He spoke with difficulty. His large frame was no longer impressive but apologetic. Putin, on the other hand, looked lean, sharp and unemotional. He promised: "There will be no power vacuum – not even for a moment."

Listening to Yeltsin's moving speech on New Year's Eve, Russians wept. In March 2000 53.4% of them voted for Putin.

Oxford, 2000-2001

Alison, my next-door neighbour at Catz, had a bread-making machine. On Sunday nights the homely smell would transform my room from a spartan student cell into a cosy nest. I would close my eyes and imagine myself back in my grandmother's kitchen with Babushka baking a tray of cabbage cake with a crusty top and soft, buttery filling. I had to remind myself that I was a poor student thousands of miles from home in a dorm with a primitive, dirty kitchen. But the smell wafting from next door was impossibly seductive. It was January 2000, sometime at the beginning of Hilary term, when I knocked on Alison's door with the thinly-veiled intention of getting a slice of her loaf.

The freshly-baked bread was resting on a rack, an opulent, golden brick with a deeper honey-coloured crust on top. Alison had just come back from a shower after a football match. Her shin pads and boots, still caked with mud and slivers of grass around the spikes, lay on the floor. I hid my impatience and asked Alison about the match, silently congratulating myself on coming up with "small talk", which appeared to be obligatory in Britain. Before I knew it, I was drawn into a conversation about football, conducted in Alison's Glaswegian accent. Alison played for Catz Birds, our College women's team, for four years and talked passionately about training and matches, obviously trying to recruit me. The women's squad needed more players and no prior experience was necessary. "Some fresh air and a bit of exercise would be good for you!" finished Alison at the end of her pitch. I found myself nodding. This is how I joined the Catz Birds. My signing bonus was a thick slice of Alison's loaf.

The following weekend I had my first taste of football. The pitch on the outskirts of Oxford was bare but the mud was firm, touched with frost. I was wearing the team's navy kit and brand-new football boots I had picked up on sale. We practised passing the ball for a bit, but Sarah, the team captain, was distracted: only ten girls had turned up that morning, with the rest of the squad probably too hung-over to climb out of bed. We faced strong opponents who had gone undefeated the previous term. Before I knew it, I was told to take position in right midfield. At once I was breathless from the icy January air surging into my lungs. I was unfit and hardly knew what I was doing, but the experience was exhilarating. I even kicked the ball once, not that it did any good. We were down by a couple of goals by halftime. Just as we were tucking into fresh orange quarters, a halftime ritual I came to love, a blonde girl with her long hair tied into a ponytail jogged up to join us. Alex had played football at school, and in addition to experience, she had attitude. She put on her boots and sprinted into the field, shouting "Show us what you've got, you cunts!" intimidating the hell out of the opposition.

We did not win that time and nor did we have a particularly successful season. Yet I found myself looking forward to every weekend, longing to put on my boots and inhale the smell of wet grass. It was also the sense of camaraderie and taking on the men's game that I found so satisfying. It did not matter that I had to stay up late on Sundays to finish my essays. Meanwhile, I was beginning to pick up on all things British, absorbing everything like a sponge. We often went for drinks after matches and I became partial to shandy. Pubs, which I had found off-putting at first because of their stained carpets and the sickly sour smell of stale beer, began to grow on me. Sometimes we went for a curry at one of Indian restaurants on Oxford's Cowley Road, which enticed students with their bring-your-own-bottle deals. I did not know my rogan josh from my tikka masala but I caught myself feeling happy in the loud company of girls with red, wind-swept cheeks. Jess, however, wasn't too impressed when I asked her: "What's a cunt?"

The following year I became the team captain. I still wasn't any good at football but I instilled pride and commitment in the squad. I appointed a PhD student as our coach and organised regular training sessions. I put a lot of effort into recruiting visiting American students to join the team, promising a "quintessential Oxford experience" by way of football curries together with the men's squad. Some American girls were fiendishly good at soccer and I took full advantage of it, sometimes at the expense of the undergraduates who diligently turned up to every practice but weren't that good. I played in defence and compensated for my lack of football skills by roaring "Come on Catz Birds!" until I lost my voice. We became a solid squad and got through to the quarter finals of Cuppers, the inter-College knock-out tournament, only to be crushed by Brasenose thanks to my pathetic own goal at the end of the match. I was devastated, but not for too long, because by that time I had also taken up rowing.

I paid twenty pounds for a nearly brand new bike from a visiting student who was going back to the States after an eight-week term. I also picked up a new electric kettle and a pair of dining plates from her hoard. American students were bright and, most importantly, seriously rich kids who were simultaneously paying overseas student fees in Oxford and US tuition fees to keep their places at the Ivy League colleges back home. The exchange students were pleased to go home, wearing Oxford sweatshirts marketed especially to them by the High Street shops, with prestigious bullet points on their CVs. I was happy I could now cycle to remote football grounds, a cheaper supermarket on the outskirts of Oxford and down to the river.

Once the cold, wet winter gave way to spring, it was not hard to fall in love with rowing. After plenty of cancelled outings (because the high water level was considered too dangerous for rowing) and miserable training sessions in the rain, rowing in Trinity term (the final term of the academic year in Oxford, which lasts from mid-April to mid-June) was the fondest memory of my life as a student. I would get up early, put on my lycra and cycle to the River Isis (part of the Thames) via Broad Street and Cornmarket, which were blissfully empty at that hour. On my way I would nod to the magnificent old Oxford Colleges: New College, Trinity, Balliol, Pembroke and Christ Church. I'd cycle down St Aldate's to the Folly Bridge and turn left onto the river path. The towpath was notoriously muddy even on a sunny day, but cycling more slowly meant taking time to inhale the aroma of fresh grass and the distinct smell of the river, peaceful but for the sound of the quacking ducks, understandably angry at the impudent rowers. I'd arrive at the Catz clubhouse by the "Gut" (a turning point of the Isis), happy and impatient to get out on the water.

The eight of us would lift a delicate boat, put it in the water and fix up the oars with pale turquoise and maroon blades, painted in St. Catherine's College colours. We'd slip into the boat and push off gently, guided by a cox. We were coached by Emily Woodeson, who in the previous term had rowed for the university in the Boat Race between Oxford and Cambridge. Oxford won. Emily taught us technique and endurance in preparation for the Summer Eights.

Summer Eights is a "bumps" race – a traditional Oxford regatta in which College boats chase each other in single file in attempt to catch and "bump" the boat in front. The races take place over four days, and the competition is organised into several divisions with the first men's and women's crews in the first division competing for a title Head of the River. Even though a typical contact between the two boats is gentle (because rowing boats cost a fortune), "bumps" races are a more exciting spectator sport than head-to-head races. Inevitably, collisions happen, ancient rivalries flare up and inept rowers commit the ultimate mistake they are desperate to avoid: "catching a crab". This happens when a rower is late lifting a blade from the water, slowing down the boat or even falling into the water to the delight of the spectators.

I wasn't particularly good at rowing, but I loved it. I became obsessed with using the indoor rowing machine, began lifting weights and never missed a practice. I adored Emily and got cross with other girls who joined the club to have fun and didn't take it seriously. During Summer Eights we shared the dining table with the senior College crews, joining them in "carb-loading" every dinner. They talked strategy and discussed the competition, while we were simply excited to be eavesdropping on their conversation. For the first time since my matriculation, I sat in the Hall, being served, rather than piling pasta and baked potatoes onto someone else's plate.

We raced in the lower division, which had fewer spectators, but it was enough to know that fellow Catz rowers watched us from the boat club by the Gut and that Emily cycled along the river, roaring support. Every race began at an overwhelming pace to get the boat started, with our pulses rocketing sky-high. The cox then guided us towards a steadier pace, focusing on powering every stroke. Our thighs were burning and we did our best to synchronise our breathing and pace. On the first day we rowed over, which meant we did not get bumped but nor were we fast enough to catch the crew in front of us. The following day we bumped a boat ahead, only to get bumped back on day three. We did well overall, given our very modest experience. I was hooked and continued to row in my final year, despite the exam pressure.

I came to love sport and amazed myself by becoming a keen runner. I had never liked running, because of the vivid memories of my childhood weekend tribulations. I took it up as a break between rowing training and to give the painful blisters on my palms a chance to heal. Soon I was going for long runs, grateful to have the freedom to enjoy the public parks. Back in Russia in the 1990s, I had avoided the park, especially in the dark. Walking on my own would be unthinkable because of lurking burglars, rapists or drug addicts. Dogs also presented a threat. As if mirroring the mood of their struggling or angry owners, dogs in Russia were always aggressive, regardless of their breed. Whenever I went running in the Oxford parks and spotted a dog, I always slowed down to a walk. It took me a couple of years to begin to trust dogs in Oxford and to use a zebra crossing without fear of being run over. Pedestrian lives weren't very precious back home.

I often had to pinch myself, so surreal was it for me to be a student at Oxford. At the end of my first year I asked my college for financial support. Officially, there weren't any bursaries available to undergraduate students, especially those from overseas. I feared I would be packing my suitcases and going back home to Russia. Fortunately, the college waived my tuition fees and then lent me the money to pay my university tuition fees for the second year. In my third year, my parents paid my college fees, and the university gave me another loan. On the one hand, I was just like any other student, going on crew dates with other colleges, getting drunk and nursing hangovers; on the other hand, I was always conscious of my good fortune. I knew I belonged in Oxford and its ancient cobbled streets, and yet it seemed as if every stone stood out to remind me of how special it was to walk on them. In practical terms, my loans were due for repayment a year after graduation. I had to find a well-paid job.

***

Every student loves a freebie. A poor student never misses one. It became a hobby of mine to attend graduate recruitment events organised by investment banks and management consultancies. We were a perfect match: City firms looked to fill their entry level positions with Oxbridge talent, while students took advantage of the free bar and nibbles. Banks and consultancies would hire the Oxford Town Hall or a similarly impressive venue and bring over their most presentable executives: men in impeccable suits and women with ostentatious leather bags. These executives were usually Oxbridge graduates themselves, who would start the night with a tale of a university rugby star turned polished banker. They'd feed our impressionable young minds with glitzy stories of business travel, transporting us to the world of five-star hotels and business lounges, obviously omitting the fact that on a typical trip to Amsterdam they would not venture outside of Schiphol airport. A management consultant in an expensive white silk blouse and a pencil skirt would then outline a typical project and explain her role on it, with the narrative resembling the plot of a Hollywood 'save the world' blockbuster. Then her male colleague, who invariably bore an uncanny resemblance to Superman when disguised in a suit and a pair of thick-rimmed glasses, would talk about the daily challenges he tackled, appealing to the ambitious, competitive nature of his audience. By that point a typical student would already be on her third glass of wine and fourth smoked salmon canapé. Sometimes I would spy my fellow Economics & Management students leeching onto the executives in the hope of pinching some interview tips. I would mock them at the next morning's lecture, but privately I too was impressed. I picked up a corporate brochure and cut out its seductive marketing slogan: "Just because you're starting at the top doesn't mean you can't go higher."

I did not know it at a time, but I got caught in a carefully designed trap. With its demanding jobs, sleek executives and shiny brochures, the City promised the world, or at least the next logical step for an Oxford student studying for a diploma in Economics & Management. The recruiters played on our ambitions and offered us the perfect new challenge. I was also very aware that I needed an employer who would sponsor my work visa for the UK and allow me to pay off my debt quickly. Just like many of my peers, I applied for summer internships during my second year. Soon I heard back from Merrill Lynch, one of the world's top investment banks at the time, and I was on my way for an interview in the City of London.

I remember walking through the maze of the City's skyscrapers, gawping around me in wonder. It must have been a Friday because most men wore pink shirts under tailored suits and carried matching pink newspapers. I pulled up the sleeve of my blazer to hide the stain on the cuff of my white waitressing shirt. The streets smelled of shoe polish, freshly made coffee and something else I could not quite place. Black cabs stopped by the grand office entrances to drop off their customers, who stepped out with a presidential air of self-importance. There was effortless synchronicity to everything and everyone, which mesmerised me. I found the Merrill Lynch building at Ropemaker Place and glanced at the dark glass panels, rising up to the sunlit sky. Next I was in a polished elevator going up to the top floor with a smart reception and an enviable view of the City.

I was interviewed by a managing director called David and was impressed (as was no doubt the intention) that such an important person had found time in his busy diary to meet a lowly student like me. He wore a navy suit, a pale pink shirt and glasses, which appeared to magnify his attentiveness to my career aspirations. In the presence of this obviously successful man, with his expensive cuff links and his assured voice, it felt as if I'd been transported from the world of carrying endless piles of dirty plates in the Catz dining hall to becoming an important voice at the negotiating table of one of the world's most sought after corporate finance advisers. I had spent the last year feeling anxious every time I withdrew cash from a bank machine and checked my account balance. Now I imagined what it might be like to stop worrying about money *at all*. At that time, it meant buying myself a new white shirt, ready meals from Marks & Spencer and going on holiday to the Black Sea. When I asked David about my work visa, he just grinned. That day I glimpsed life in *Merrillland* through a polished rabbit hole and saw nothing but a splendid garden. I fell for it and was delighted when Merrill Lynch offered me a paid summer internship.

London, summer 2001

My internship began in July 2001, right after the Henley regatta where my college crew had entered an amateur race. In the City of London, no one cared about blades and accolades: the purpose of the eight-week program was to get a job offer by September. There were about thirty of us: penultimate year students from Europe's top universities, hungry to prove ourselves. There were tailor-dressed economists from Paris and Milan, already looking every inch the City executives, shy mathematicians from Oxford, hoping to impress with their numbers skills, and gregarious engineers from Cambridge, who made friends effortlessly by reminding bankers of their frivolous student days. In the first week we received training in Excel, PowerPoint and corporate finance. At night we were taken out for drinks at the City's rooftop bars. On Friday we were shown our desks in an open-plan office and allocated our first projects.

Underneath the client floor, the Merrill Lynch office was a shabby place, infested with mice and illuminated by artificial light – day and night. There were piles of old presentations, research reports and newspapers stacked everywhere, while acrylic artefacts, commemorating closed deals, gathered dust on office desks. I joined the team of an Italian associate and a French analyst working on a client pitch for that Monday. In contrast to the highly publicised meritocracy in all the brochures, investment banking is extremely hierarchical. At the top of the pyramid are managing directors courting corporate clients, directors leading the projects, vice presidents (or VPs) managing the day-to-day process, associates taking on interesting tasks and checking the rest of the work produced by analysts. Analysts are the ones who build financial models, conduct research, crunch numbers, put together presentations and write documents, be it press releases or IPO prospectuses. They are also good at fetching fresh bagels from Brick Lane and carrying pitch books. These are strange people, surviving on virtually no sleep, fuelled by caffeine and deeply troubled by rapid transformation from academic stars to obliging minions. Of course, on that Friday I only saw what I wanted to see: an Excel virtuoso who taught me basic spreadsheet skills and kindly showed me how to order pizza on the corporate account, a standard practice when working late.

I worked until midnight that Friday and for twelve hours straight on Saturday. On Sunday I was allowed to take the afternoon off to move from the hotel by St. Paul's, paid for by Merrill Lynch, to a student dorm in Bethnal Green, where I would spend the summer in a poky, spartan room. I don't remember, but the meeting might well have been cancelled or postponed to another Monday, which meant that some juniors would spend another weekend updating the numbers and the slides for the presentation because of a late meeting arrangement or because someone at the top of the hierarchy forgot to delegate work until the last minute. It happened often enough but analysts did not complain. Nor did summer interns, who were just grateful to be there and desperate to please.

Whether I slept for six hours or three, I always made it to the office by nine o'clock. I took cold showers to help me wake up and plastered on make-up to hide the dark circles under my eyes. If the contrast between the slums of Bethnal Green and the skyline of Liverpool Street Station on my way to the office was startling, I was too tired to notice it. As a paid intern, I could now afford to buy Starbucks coffee and so I savoured little pleasures such as a frothy cappuccino and a still-warm croissant for breakfast. I would bring a half-litre paper cup of coffee to my desk and begin the day by comparing notes with fellow summer interns. I remember Tariq guzzling two energy drink cans in a row and telling us about "doing a model" all night long with relish, as if he was referring to a sexual conquest. For Tariq and everyone else, an "all-nighter" was just another obstacle in the game of endurance which a high-achiever had no choice but to tackle head on.

It was Andrew, a VP in the Mergers and Acquisitions team, who advised us to be at our desks by nine in his welcome speech at the beginning of the summer programme. "As analysts, you are expected to be on time, especially if you are staffed on a public transaction. Flick through the *FT*, read the *Lex* column, check *Bloomberg* and be ready," preached Andrew. He had strawberry-blond hair, pale blue eyes and a surprisingly healthy complexion for a thirty-year-old banker. Most of his peers looked at least a decade older than their age, losing hair and supporting their protruding guts with braces. Andrew, it was rumoured, had been busy checking a merger document in the office when his wife gave birth to their first child. He was a stickler for detail, as I discovered one morning. He asked me to compile a pack of information on Tempus, a media-buying agency listed on the London Stock Exchange. I piled together annual reports, brokers' notes, share price data and bound the documents. I put the latest press cuttings on the takeover offer for Tempus by Havas, a large advertising group, at the front of the pack. The offer valued Tempus at £425 million and generated a lot of publicity, with the company's share price soaring through the roof. Andrew summoned me to his desk and said: "I know they teach you to show initiative at Oxford, but here we need you to do as you are told. Take it back and give me the pack with the annual report filed upfront."

My blunder aside, I was very excited to be staffed on a live deal, which was every analyst's dream. Another advertising group, WPP, hired Merrill Lynch and Goldman Sachs to advise it on making a rival bid for Tempus. The bankers' job was to come up with the right offer price and then manage the acquisition process. In August 2001, WPP announced a higher offer for Tempus, trumping the earlier bid by ten million pounds, and the battle commenced. A contested deal for a publicly listed company is pretty much as exciting as it gets in the M&A (mergers and acquisitions) world. Every morning I read a new article on the deal, proud to be associated with it. Even as a summer intern, I was tasked with proofing the offer document and analysing share trading volumes – simple, but meaningful tasks. The deal team took me to a press conference where Martin Sorrell, the CEO of WPP, explained the deal rationale to financial journalists and research analysts. WPP won the contest (even if it later tried to back out of the deal), and I found myself hooked on the adrenaline of the deal frenzy.

Long nights in the office were intermittently sweetened with lavish dinners and parties. Investment banks took their summer interns to London's most fashionable restaurants for intimate dinners with senior executives. I sat next to David, the managing director who had interviewed me, and told him about my experience on a live deal over a starter of scallops, a dish I had copied him in ordering. I sipped a champagne cocktail and looked glamorous in my new dress from Karen Millen, a high-street brand I could only have dreamed of wearing before. It did not matter that on the way back to Bethnal Green I ruined the pleated silk in the rain; the taste of luxury lingered on.

At the end of the summer I flew to Ekaterinburg to spend time with my family. My grandmother Tonya was so poorly, she could no longer leave her bed and was suffering terribly. I was desperate to see her. I called her from London often, but the sight of her, so frail and feeble, unsettled me. She was propped up on her sofa bed with the cushions she had embroidered herself. One cushion had an asymmetric pattern, because even though Baba Tonya's eyes had failed her, she had stubbornly finished her craftwork. Behind the sofa the carpet hung on the wall in the old Soviet fashion, but the small bedroom no longer looked cosy. Now it was suffocating with the smell of dirty linen, sickness and despair. I tried to sound upbeat and talked about London, my internship and the job offer I hoped to receive. Baba Tonya nodded, her lips relaxing into something I was determined to read as a smile. I sensed that she had fought her illness with single-minded resolve to see me again and now she felt content. As if reading my mind, she said: "Now I can die in peace."

Just as I was fighting back tears to protest, she smiled in earnest and asked me if I wanted *pel'meni*. *Pel'meni* are the Russian equivalent of Chinese dumplings, Italian tortellini, Ukrainian *vareniki*, Georgian *khinkali*, Japanese *gyōza* and Tibetan *momos*: thin pastry parcels filled with meat, vegetables or mushrooms. In Russia, *pel'meni* is the traditional dish of the Urals and Siberia, cooked with minced beef, pork or even bear meat. Making *pel'meni* is a ritual in which the whole family takes part. Each member is assigned a particular task and it becomes a social occasion, with gossip exchanged, ailments discussed and remedies recalled. Perhaps it's what makes this relatively simple dish so special.

During my childhood, no dish delighted me as much as *pel'meni* with cabbage, made by Baba Tonya. It was the humblest of recipes but each parcel was filled with love. Babushka made her own pastry, mixing white flour, water and eggs and kneading it on her kitchen table. She had a big wooden dish with a concave base to match the shape of the heavy, club-shaped *sechka* she used to finely dice the cabbage and then season it with hot butter and salt.

Once the pastry was ready, Baba Tonya would cut a chunk and roll it into a long sausage. Even as a child, I would be entrusted with a knife to cut the sausage into inch-sized pieces, before squashing them with my thumb on a flour-dusted board. The next step was too tricky for a child to accomplish, especially as Baba Tonya had to have it just so. She used a small rolling pin to form wafer-thin, perfectly round discs. If the discs were too thin, the *pel'meni* would break in the boiling water, while thick discs were frowned upon, silently branding their maker "unskilled". Then Babushka would put a heaped teaspoon of cabbage on top of each disc, fold it and seal it with her nimble fingers. Each piece always looked neat and identical, despite her ailing eyesight. She served her *pel'meni* with thick sour cream, and I ate plate after plate until I was fit to burst, because a show of poor appetite was sure to offend.

When Baba Tonya mentioned *pel'meni*, I was momentarily confused, because it was clear that she could not have made them herself and she'd never touch the ready-made *pel'meni* from the supermarket.

"*Pel'meni?*" Even as I said the word, I felt my mouth watering.

"Yes, the carer made them," she replied, "are you hungry?"

"*Da…*"

It turned out that Baba Tonya had instructed her carer to make *pel'meni* that morning, guiding her through the process, step-by-step, from her bed. The carer cooked them for us and brought me a plate into the bedroom. I balanced the plate on my lap and began to eat.

"Are they tasty?" Baba Tonya asked me.

"They're good, but not as good as yours," I replied. In truth, they were too salty because of the hot tears streaming down onto my plate.

***

Baba Tonya died two weeks later and was buried next to her husband. On a few occasions, I asked my mother to make *pel'meni* with cabbage for me, but somehow they never tasted quite right.

Chapter XI in which fresh meat was cooked to perfection

The 2000s created an illusion of stability and prosperity in Russia. While the Kremlin didn't introduce any reforms to stimulate the real economy, focussing instead on safeguarding macroeconomic stability and budgetary discipline, oil prices began to rise and Russia's economic growth surged. As a result, disposable incomes rose and people's lives flourished. Finally, Russians were prospering and enjoying a restored sense of stability and pride. In exchange, the Kremlin did not ask for much, just that people stayed out of politics.

People cheered when Putin cracked down on the oligarchs, arresting Mikhail Khodorkovsky, Russia's richest man, in 2003, and in doing so sending a powerful signal to other business tycoons. Oligarchs learned their lesson quickly and either kowtowed to the president or fled the country.

By 2002, the State controlled all the main television channels after oligarchs Berezovsky and Gusinsky sold their stakes in ORT and NTV respectively. The independent media channels, which dared to challenge the Kremlin, were forced into line or simply shut down. Unsuitable current affairs programmes, such as *Namedni,* were taken off air.

In September 2004 Putin announced a series of reforms to centralise power in order to "enhance national cohesion". Regional governors were no longer elected but appointed by the Kremlin; parliamentary candidates, unaffiliated with any party, were discouraged from standing.

The Duma, already controlled by Putin's party, United Russia, endorsed the new laws.

21 December 2002, London

I jumped out of the cab on New Bond Street and ran down a narrow cobbled lane, decorated with garlands of festive lights. Jess had suggested a trendy bar tucked away in a Mayfair mews to celebrate my birthday and said she would invite along a few university friends. I could not wait to see them and tried to picture George, the god of fancy dress, now clad in a suit. I wondered if the party animals Dom and Jo would be there. Most of all I was looking forward to buying a round of drinks for my friends, now that I was no longer skint. "I might splash out on a bottle of *Veuve Clicquot!*" I thought to myself, as I opened the door and thrust my bag in the air: "Ta da!"

The bar was empty, except for a barman, impatiently wiping the tables, and Jess, who wore an apologetic smile on her face.

"Where is everyone?"

"Darling, it's nearly eleven," said Jess patiently.

"Fuck… I am sorry, I just could not get out of the office," I said, dropping down onto the nearest chair. "And yes I know it's a fucking Saturday!" I added furiously, then pressed my palms to my face as if to restrain myself. "I am sorry."

"Darling, I love you, but I've got catch a train to Haywards Heath," said Jess, who was heading home for Christmas.

"I know, it's my fault," I sighed. "Merry Christmas." We hugged and she was off.

I turned to the barman: "May I…?"

"Go on then," he sighed too, but not without sympathy.

I ordered a glass of champagne and stared at the bubbles. I opened a few cards, unwrapped Jess's present and burst into tears. Half an hour earlier, I had been in the office, working on a pitch for an insurance company. It was potentially a huge mandate for Merrill Lynch, and there was no sign of anyone there winding down for Christmas. At the eleventh hour, a managing director on the project had had a light-bulb moment and emailed the pitch team saying: "Could we see if the presentation would look better in A3 rather than A4 format?" As a consequence, I spent Saturday reorganising charts, tables and text boxes into the larger slides and simply couldn't leave the office until I had circulated the new draft.

I left the bar dejected and headed to Oxford Street to catch a bus home. The magic of the Christmas lights taunted my eyes, which were sore from the hours in front of a computer screen. I bought a tub of Ben & Jerry's ice cream at a corner shop and threw it on the bed at home. I looked at my reflection in the mirror. I had put on weight, my skin looked unhealthy, and the dark circles under my eyes were obvious, despite the industrial-strength concealer smeared over them. My long blonde hair looked lifeless, like sun-bleached seaweed. My shoulders were stooped and ached from stress and tension. I felt and looked terrible.

How did this happen to me?

***

June 2002, Oxford

Six months earlier I had been sitting on the pavement by the Sheldonian Theatre, drinking Tesco's finest champagne straight from the bottle. I wore *sub fusc* and a red carnation, clipped to my chest as a symbol of my last Finals exam. My hair was sticky from the sparkling wine sprayed over my head by friends who came to meet me and others at the Exam Schools. I was covered in confetti and paper ribbons and sported a large grin. I had finished my Finals and I was celebrating! I peaked too early and ended up in bed by eight o'clock that evening with my sheets awash with confetti.

Jess, Tim and Hairy Matt were staying in Oxford to do Masters in Economics. I imagined them growing stale in the library and feeling their age when Oxford filled up with the new intake of Freshers. I loved Oxford, but I was ready for a new challenge: the City of London. Merrill Lynch had offered me a job and I grabbed the opportunity. We, the newly recruited analysts from Europe and the US, were to be sent to New York for a five-week training programme. I had never been to the States before. "Darling, you must go to Bloomingdale's!" said Jess on our last night out in Oxford. As I stripped the sheets from the single bed in my St. Catherine's cell, my mind was already elsewhere.

July 2002, New York

The apartment hotel where we stayed for the summer was just opposite Madison Square Gardens in Manhattan. Its lobby was always busy with holidaymakers – Americans, relaxed in white t-shirts, and Europeans, enduring the heat in their best clothes. The incessant hum of the air-conditioning competed with the zing of the elevators, the ring of reception telephones and the tireless hotel staff, bossing the tourists around. The kaleidoscope of uniformed bellboys, yellow cabs and multi-coloured shopping bags rotated around the clock, mesmerising all the first-time visitors to New York.

In the mornings, my cohort of young investment bankers, overly fastidious about their attire and much too careless with their money because of the sign-on bonuses we had received, hailed cabs to take us to Wall Street. On the client floor of the Merrill Lynch office we enjoyed a lavish breakfast buffet of fresh bagels, smoked salmon, roast beef and cream cheese. We pumped ourselves with coffee to counter the effects of late night partying and began training. We learned about accounting and finance and how to value companies. We were drilled in Excel and PowerPoint. Senior bankers came to address us, instilling in us the importance of upholding a culture of excellence, and we believed them, because now *we* were *them*. The first-class training programme was gruelling but on weekends we explored New York and could not believe our luck. When I heard I had got a First in my Finals, I hardly paid attention. I was climbing a new Everest now, in a new fitted white shirt I had bought in Bloomingdale's.

September 2002 – June 2005, London

After the training in New York, I flew to London and received some time off to settle in and study for regulatory exams. I found a freshly renovated studio flat in Notting Hill in

West London and moved in. It was pretty but tiny, just seventeen square metres, but I soon discovered that I would be spending little time at home anyway. In the mornings, it took me about ten minutes to walk to Notting Hill Gate tube station, and I treasured every step of what I thought of as my only experience of a normal life. Local residents walked their dogs, parents took their children to school. On weekends, I had to weave my way through a crowd of tourists coming to hunt for bargains at the Portobello Road market. I remember that once I spotted a Merrill Lynch colleague coming out of Starbucks on Westbourne Grove, and stopping by a dustbin to throw away his pocketful of coins. Perhaps Notting Hill was not normal after all, or maybe it was tarnished by the bankers who lived there.

On the tube, I always tried to sit by the glass partition so I could lean my head against it and catch up on some sleep. (Amazingly, I only missed my stop once.) I'd get out at St. Paul's and cross the road to the new Merrill Lynch office. It was a brand new building rising to just six floors, a respectful nod to the nearby Sir Christopher Wren masterpiece. Its lobby was tastefully decorated with walnut wood, marble floors and a glazed ceiling, which extended across the entire office. When I first set my eyes on it, I thought I'd arrived. But after a couple of days of welcome speeches and compliance training, followed by obligatory drinks on the roof terrace, the honeymoon period was over. The reality of life as a junior investment banker crushed any illusions I may have harboured.

I was assigned to a Financial Institutions Group, which advised banks, insurance and asset management companies on raising capital and M&A (mergers and acquisitions). In the early days, I would arrive on the fifth floor and greet everyone with a cheerful "Good morning!" but I soon stopped when I realised that no one ever replied. If anything, my colleagues, sitting in an open plan office, seemed to hunch their shoulders and lean closer to their monitors to appear busy. It was autumn 2002 and redundancies were in full swing. It was common to be working on a project with an associate who would give me an assignment one evening, only for me to discover his desk eerily empty the next morning. People disappeared all the time and I never saw them again. Fortunately, I did not read *1984* until much later, so I wasn't spooked. Besides, as junior analysts we were cheap and therefore enjoyed job security. I could not say the same about the job itself.

My team was frantically pitching for business to every financial institution in Europe. This meant that I spent about one hundred hours in the office each week working on one hundred-page presentations. In my team, juniors were never taken to client meetings, so for the first six months I survived on the mistaken belief that my work mattered. Once I was assigned to work on a pitch led by a managing director called Charles (not his real name). At first I felt jubilant: working directly for a senior banker was a privilege. Very soon I discovered that I was as naive as a lamb arriving at the slaughterhouse. Charles came out of his office with his hands on his head, his eyes rolling in agony. He had a light scar on his face, which always turned crimson when he was stressed.

On this occasion, Charles had the appearance of a man who had just lost everything on the stock market, with his children now doomed to a life of poverty. In actual fact, Charles had just remembered to review a draft of a presentation ahead of a client meeting the following day. His secretary summoned me into his office. It was petrifying. He made me sit as he continued to read the slides in silence, occasionally giving a dramatic sigh. Eventually he looked up at me and said: "I've got nothing to present. Five acquisition targets? I need twenty-five. 8 o'clock tomorrow." His secretary popped in to tell him he was late for lunch. "It's a disaster," he complained to her, pointing at me. "I don't reckon I'll be back today," he added, no doubt looking forward to a long boozy lunch. I felt sick anticipating the enormity of the task ahead and desperately needed more guidance, but I didn't dare speak up. I often saw Charles in Notting Hill, taking his son to a primary school and appearing to be an affectionate father, but as soon as he got to the City, Dr. Jekyll turned into Mr. Hyde.

In November I had my graduation ceremony in Oxford. My parents travelled from Russia to share the joyous celebration with me. At the time I was working on a pitch to a Scandinavian bank and had to beg to be allowed to meet my parents at the airport on the Friday night. On Saturday we went to Oxford for the day. I was exhausted. With my puffy, spotted face I looked as if I had just pulled through after a grave illness. My parents were shocked to see me so worn out just a few months after starting work. In the evening we had to return to London because I had to go to the office on Sunday. They could not understand it and we argued. How could I explain to them that my dream job was killing me, when I could hardly come to terms with it myself?

At night I always took a cab back home. It was on a

corporate account. I'd open the door and collapse on the back seat, grateful to add twenty minutes of sleep to a few hours at home. Occasionally I could enjoy one day off on the weekend. I would wake up in a dreadful state even after ten hours of sleep and go to Selfridges. I'd buy myself a designer bag or a pair shoes, stupidly hoping it would make me feel better. I would meet up with friends in the evening, but gradually they stopped asking me out because I usually cancelled on them. I became an unhappy, easily irritated person. I'd be rude to cab drivers and shop assistants, as if they were to blame for my self-inflicted circumstances. Svetlana, my friend from the German boarding school, told me I'd changed. I did not like it one bit. I was meant to be clever, rich and successful, not an arsehole.

**

Every phone call to my parents ended up with me feeling frustrated and misunderstood. I'd end up sulking, even though it was me who was unable to open up to them properly and share my anguish. Instead, I often called my school friend Anya, who lived in a completely different world from mine, yet always found time to listen to me. Anya worked in political PR and then marketing in Ekaterinburg. She lived with her long-term boyfriend, who was a professional basketball player. Their kitchen in a tiny tower block flat in an obscure neighbourhood was the most welcoming place in the city, with friends, neighbours and near strangers frequently popping in, as long as they had a story to tell. Every time I came back to Ekaterinburg, I headed to Anya's and set up camp on a stool by the kitchen table. (Anya always perched with a cigarette by the window, which was opened even in winter, inevitably killing even the sturdiest home plants.) Next, Anya's friend Elena would turn up and tell us about her latest crush. Then Pasha, who worked in the police force, would shower us with anecdotes from his recent shift and bring an expensive bottle of cognac, presumably confiscated. Anya's boyfriend would come home later after training, take a bottle of vodka out of the freezer and insist I match him shot for shot as he filled me in on what had been happening in Moscow and regional politics. Throughout the night new characters would walk in with beer, rye bread and *shproty* – tinned sprats in oil, once a delicacy produced in Latvia and shipped all over the USSR for festive occasions. Anya's kitchen on such nights was indeed packed like a tin of sprats. We always ended up talking well into the night, eating and drinking. I'd sleep at Anya's and wake up demanding *rassol*, leftover brine, a reliable Russian remedy to reduce the inevitable suffering from the night before.

I'd call Anya from London and pour out my troubles, imagining myself sitting in her kitchen, which was the antipode of the Merrill Lynch office. Her own life was in chaos, with her boyfriend transferring to another city thousands of miles away from Ekaterinburg, her father's entanglement in local politics, and her longing for a child, but nothing seemed to ruffle her much. Perhaps, like most Russians, she was used to the turbulence of daily life or perhaps her busy kitchen helped her to put the world to rights.

***

In those days I rarely left the Merrill Lynch building. Socialising was confined to the office canteen and when I sought counselling, I turned to Lars (not his real name), a managing director who had been appointed as my mentor at work. We would sit down in his office, with Lars behind his desk, flicking through emails while I spoke. I told him that I had not yet had a chance to build a model. Male analysts in my year often boasted about building complicated models during our dinners at the office canteen, while female analysts were usually asked to put together glossy presentations. I too wanted to get stuck into a meatier type of work. My mentor nodded, which gave me a flicker of hope.

A month later I had my first appraisal with Lars. He pointed out a major flaw in my performance to date: "You haven't yet built a model! Didn't they teach you anything in New York?"

The Human Resources department was too busy firing people to help. Still, they did what they could. They organised lectures on work-life balance, which took place in the evenings. After lectures we'd go back to our desks to catch up on the lost time and ended up working past midnight. I resented women who worked in HR. They looked so healthy and polished. They floated by our desks on the way to meet a senior banker to discuss the next round of redundancies, looking utterly serene.

Sometimes the HR people got lucky. Rather than waiting to be fired, bankers beat them to it by dying instead. One analyst in my team was diagnosed with leukaemia and never recovered. Then an associate dropped dead after a heart attack. Years later, a retired head of the Financial Institutions

Group hired a gallery in Mayfair to display a collection of his photographs of autumn leaves, a contemplation of beauty and death.

***

In June, first-year analysts received their bonuses and a few brave souls handed in their resignation letters. We all suffered from the punishing hours, meaningless work and heartless superiors, but it took guts to walk away. For a high achiever with a stellar academic record and an exemplary career path, it was unthinkable to admit defeat. A few of us junior bankers were sitting in the corner of a pub called The Butcher's Hook & Cleaver, nursing pints of lager. The pub was one of many watering holes in the City, just a few minutes' walk away from the Merrill Lynch office by the Smithfield meat market.

"I've seen myself working in the City since I was sixteen," said Marcus, "My father's a banker – I've been reading the *FT* since I was ten. I'd be a fucking disappointment if I quit."

"I know", chimed in Dave, who used to play rugby at university, "All my mates are jealous of me landing a job in the City. If I leave, they'll think I'm a loser."

"It's got to get better," said Nick, nodding as he spoke, as if to convince himself. "What about you, Baker? Are you resigning?"

Jane Baker was a nickname given to me by my monolingual British mates.

"Nah", I sighed, playing with my business card, which had the Merrill Lynch bull embossed on its thick paper. "I've used up my bonus to pay off my student loan, and I'm on a work visa, remember? I'm chained to the bull for a while longer," I said, draining my pint and heading back to the office.

After a year in the Financial Institutions Group I asked to be transferred to the M&A team, where I hoped to be working on deals rather than endless pitches. The M&A team had a reputation for working hard and playing hard. For a junior banker it meant occasionally finishing work before 9pm and joining senior colleagues in the pub for a few rounds of drinks. Soon such drinks became routine because making any other evening plans was impossible. A "Quick drink?" became a soothing balm between stressful days and sleepless nights. Unsurprisingly, we only ever talked about work: deals, mandates, clients and colleagues. M&A bankers loosened their Hermès ties and drank six pints a night. They bitched and ranted, sneered and gossiped. I joined in, desperate to belong. Senior bankers picked juniors they liked to work on their deals. They'd say: "I want Dave because he is ace with numbers", but it surely helped that Dave was good sport in the pub when the rugby was on. During my time at Merrill Lynch I had very little idea of what was happening in Russia or on the Moon, but I became adept at talking shop, football and even clay pigeon shooting. I did not care about Russia – I wanted to be "one of the lads".

I bought pinstriped suits and double-cuffed shirts. I had my hair chopped short. I drank pints. I roared with laughter at the jokes ridiculing female directors at Merrill Lynch. "Arabella should stick to retail deals, the only industry she knows about", sniggered her male colleagues and I echoed them. I felt no affinity to the few women who had managed to climb to the top at Merrill Lynch. Perhaps, unlike men, they felt precarious rather than magnanimous in their positions of power. They kept to themselves and appeared unapproachable and even intimidating. One female managing director was especially frightening. She was tall and stern, towering above many male colleagues like a warrior queen. Bankers dreaded working for her and used her as a proverbial witch to scare the juniors. I once shared a lift with her and felt like a ferret, doomed to be eaten alive by a cobra. It seems silly: I'd never even spoken to her. Looking back, she was probably just lonely and miserable.

***

Sleep was everything in those days: a necessity and a luxury. I moved to Clerkenwell, a short walk from the office, so I could add a precious hour to my time in bed. A couple of nights a week I would walk home at 3 o'clock in the morning through the arcade of Smithfield market, with butchers unloading crates of meat in preparation for the wholesale trade. Sometimes I'd have to step over a chicken drumstick or walk around a pool of blood, but I did not mind. The butchers always said hello to me and I lived for these briefest of encounters. They made me feel I was still a person, not just a cog in the Merrill Lynch machine. On my way back to the office a few hours later, I'd find the pavement washed clean, the butchers relaxing at a nearby greasy spoon, which was proudly serving a full English with the freshest sausages in London.

I discovered another way to bolster my sleep. Merrill Lynch had a gym, which few first-year analysts had been to, but in my second year I found out about lunchtime yoga classes, taught by a softly-spoken girl. I popped down when I could, spread a mat on the floor and took a *savasana*, a corpse pose, lying on my back with my limbs spread loosely and my eyes closed. I would spend the entire class in *savasana*, often dozing off, and the teacher did not mind. Sometimes I had enough energy to circle my ankles or stretch my arms. If I opened my eyes, I found most bankers lying in *savasana*, resting in peace in an improvised graveyard.

***

As "one of the lads" on the M&A team, I was soon being staffed on deals and spent my nights building financial models and my days writing press releases and investor presentations. I bullied lawyers and accountants, helped to schmooze clients and went to boozy lunches with document printing firms who hoped to solicit Merrill Lynch business. I was back in the deal frenzy and came to enjoy myself, much like a butcher who takes pride in trimming the meat, oblivious to its smell or the ethics of animal slaughter.

In spring 2005 Merrill Lynch was invited to take part in a so-called beauty parade of investment banks to pitch for the mandate to help spin off several electricity generating assets from a giant Russian energy company. The energy sector in the Soviet Union was a fully integrated monopoly, but in 1992 state-owned assets were incorporated into a holding company, Unified Energy System, which was listed on the Russian Stock Exchange. The state retained a 50% stake in the holding. The government of Russia seemed to have been finally persuaded to liberalise the energy sector by the record cold winter of 2005, when the obsolete infrastructure caused power shortages in Moscow, St. Petersburg and the Urals. The model I had been building under the supervision of Excel fanatic Nils assumed that the spun off generators would be able to charge market prices, on the back of the anticipated Russian energy reform. I was pleased to be involved in a Russian project and worked hard to earn a place on the team travelling to Moscow to present the pitch. When Nils had a tantrum about the wrong shade of green I had used to indicate links in my Excel model, I stayed up until 2 a.m. diligently changing the colour.

I found Moscow unrecognisable. I had first laid my eyes on it when I was six. My childhood memories amounted to polishing off a revered Eskimo (chocolate-covered ice cream on a stick) and waiting to see Grandpa Lenin at the mausoleum. During the long hours in the queue, I had recited all the stories about Lenin I had learned to read with. There was one about young Lenin and his siblings preparing for their mother's birthday. Volodya made a birdhouse and I wanted one too. Then there was another story about Lenin in prison: he had been writing revolutionary messages using milk instead of ink contained in a pot he had made from bread. His wife would hold a candle underneath his letters to reveal secret instructions. Like every Soviet child, I had to do the same and wrote secret messages to my mum, who then scolded me for wasting food. The yellow waxy figure inside the mausoleum paled in comparison with these colourful stories. Much later I visited Moscow again in the dark days of the financial crisis. The Moscow of 1998 was a coil of angry queues at banks and foreign currency exchanges.

In 2005 we arrived at the renovated airport and were taken to the swanky Ararat Part Hyatt hotel. Inside there was an aura of punctilious luxury, with a chamber orchestra playing in the lobby. The hotel was situated only a few minutes' walk from Red Square. In 2005 Lenin's mausoleum was once again opened to visitors, but now it attracted only a few die-hard communists and foreign tourists. The real magnet was the new underground shopping centre nearby, with its glamorous fashion boutiques.

The client meeting took place the next day. To our surprise, our competitors, Goldman Sachs and other leading investment banks, had been invited to come to the Unified Energy System offices at the very same time. Soon it became clear that the management was using this as a tactic to let us take a good sniff at each other. After letting the bankers wait in the boardroom for a good while, the Russian clients finally graced us with their presence. They wore impeccably tailored suits and freshly polished shoes. When they addressed us, they looked at no one in particular, as if we were mere serfs, too lowly for their gaze. Instead of letting us pitch, the clients asked us to refine our valuation first. They flung some folders on the table, as a master would throw bones to a pack of dogs. The Russians knew that Merrill Lynch and Goldman Sachs would tear each other's throats to win the succulent mandate. They postponed the meetings by a month, relishing their power. Watching them check the time on their enormous Swiss watches, I felt embarrassed, but I also understood. Russia had suffered humiliation, defaulting on its debt and losing face with foreign investors in 1998, and it must have felt good to enjoy the change of fortune in the early noughties.

The Unified Energy System eventually span off its power generating subsidiaries in 2007 but I cannot tell you who won the advisory mandates. In the summer 2005 I resigned from Merrill Lynch. After three years in the bullpen, I was finally off the hook.

Chapter XII in which I travelled East

In early 2008, Russia declared support for the nationalists of Abkhazia and South Ossetia, small regions in the Caucasus, which had become parts of Georgia after the dissolution of the Soviet Union in 1991. Russians, Georgians, Ossetians and Abkhazi had lived side by side for generations. Russia's support for national separatists was the Kremlin's response to Georgia's application to join NATO. This had been brokered by the US, keen to protect its Caspian oil pipeline, which ran from Azerbaijan through Georgia, bypassing Russia and the Middle East. In August 2008, national separatists rose up, demanding independence from Georgia, and were brutally put down by the Georgian government. The Kremlin retaliated by sending in Russian forces.

For the first time since the end of the Cold War, the US poked the Russian bear, condemning its "military aggression" and "invasion of Georgia". The relations between Russia and the West have been tense ever since.

Meanwhile, the global financial crisis, which began in 2008, hit Russia hard. The stock markets plummeted, and the country's structurally weak economy, dependent on natural resource exports, fell into recession.

London, 2005 – 2009

> "When were women first allowed to vote in the UK?"
> "Er... Not sure..."
> "Where is Sutton Hoo?"

"In Hertfordshire, I think?"

"What percentage of the British population is Muslim?"

"What? I don't know!"

"I can give you multiple choice: 3%, 4%, 5% or 6%. What's your answer?"

"6%? What is this?!"

"It's 5%. Women were allowed to vote in 1918 and Sutton Hoo is in Suffolk. It's an Anglo-Saxon burial site. James, I really don't think you'd pass the *Life in the UK* test if you had to sit it…"

I was having brunch with my friend James, whom I always thought of as a quintessential Englishman. He was born and bred in Britain. James was shrewd and read the papers. He educated me about mortgages. He talked about moving to the country and although I had probably never seen him wearing tweed, I could easily imagine him dressed like a country squire, complete with a pipe and a golden retriever by his side. James always spoke with a deliberate English accent and sometimes teased me when I mispronounced words such as "oven", mimicking my elongated "o", as in "open". I was grateful for his corrections, but now it was my chance to get back at him. The *Life in the UK* test was a mandatory part of my application for British citizenship. Passing the test without studying was impossible, especially because of some of its treacherous numbers questions, which were made more difficult *because* not *despite* of the multiple-choice answers. One simply had to memorise the statistics from the study guide and practise a lot. It did not require knowledge or even fluency in English.

"I have one final question for you, James: 'Britain is proud of its record of welcoming migrants, who add to the diversity and dynamism of our national life. True or False?'"

***

After I left Merrill Lynch, I got a job at a small corporate finance advisory firm, specialising in the media sector. Its office was in Covent Garden opposite the Freemason's Hall. I found myself in a completely different environment, with friendly colleagues and manageable hours. With my training and deal experience, I was thrown in at the deep end and given more responsibility than I had ever hoped for. I relished that. I also discovered there was life outside the office; indeed, it was right on its doorstep with the National Theatre across the Waterloo Bridge, Stanford's travel book store down Long Acre, and CityLit with its evening and weekend learning courses just around the corner. Why, I even stumbled upon the Royal Opera House walking down Bow Street. Merrill Lynch soon became a distant memory, like a bad dream I hastened to forget.

***

It was at that time that a former FSB (Federal Security Service, the successor of the Soviet KGB) officer, Alexander Litvinenko, was poisoned with polonium and died in London. It was revealed that he had fled Russia and been granted political asylum in Britain. It was alleged but never proven that his death had been ordered directly by President Putin. According to the Western media, Litvinenko claimed that the

FSB had been responsible for the Moscow apartment block bombings in 1999 and for the murder of the journalist Anna Politkovskaya in October 2006. Russian media suggested it was Boris Berezovsky, a dissident oligarch residing in London, who was responsible for the murder of Litvinenko. I found myself in the middle of the media crossfire. I felt sorry for the man and his family; it was clear he had been killed in the most cruel and painful way, but he didn't seem an innocent victim to me. He had worked for the FSB and he had defected. It was possible that he was a traitor, selling Russian state secrets to MI6 or that he did some shady work for Berezovsky. After all, how could a former Russian government employee afford to pay for a townhouse in Muswell Hill and send his son to a private school? In 2006 I sided with the Russian version of the story. At the time, it was unthinkable to believe that Putin himself had ordered to silence Litvinenko, let alone that the Kremlin had been responsible for the explosions in Moscow apartment blocks.

***

In the summer 2007 my firm was acquired by a large American investment bank, which wanted to enhance its expertise in the media sector. The founders of the firm cashed in, threw a party and even shared some of their spoils with the rest of the team. The team, however, was far from overjoyed. Soon we moved into a large, lifeless office on the outskirts of the City of London. The media team was allocated a windowless open space decorated with grey carpets and matching grey furniture. Desk clusters were divided into cubicles with maroon-coloured partitions. I hated being back in the City: I felt suffocated without windows, but it was the mock opulence of the maroon by way of its association with burgundy wine or rich stage curtains that made me loathe the new employer. In no time I was back where I'd started, with long nights fuelled by Red Bull, impudent clients, impossible deadlines and weekends in the office. I decided I was through with banking.

By 2007 I had been on holidays to Thailand, Peru, Morocco, Cuba and Tibet and had caught the travel bug. However tempting it was to quit my job, I felt it was more sensible to stay put until I became a British citizen. A British passport meant independence from work visas and greater choice when it came to looking for jobs. It was also a golden ticket for an avid traveller, unrestricted by visas. Every Russian living in London can tell dozens of stories of queuing for hours in the rain outside the French Consulate just to go to Paris for a weekend. Every application was a humiliating experience, requiring bank statements, letters from an employer, proof of travel and accommodation, and insurance policies – all photocopied twice and examined by a fearsome French bureaucrat, who could, on a particularly miserable day, find fault in your passport photo and send you away. And so I stayed in banking for two more years, faking my enthusiasm for leveraged buyouts and dreaming of Kamchatka. A hook-shaped peninsula in the far east of Russia, legendary for its untouched beauty, embodied the freedom for which I yearned.

I passed the *Life in the UK* test and in 2008 I became eligible to apply for British citizenship. It was an expensive and a burdensome process but I finally I found myself in Islington Town Hall, swearing an oath of allegiance to Her Majesty the Queen. The significance of the occasion caught up with me on the day. There I was among a dozen Filipinos and a couple of Americans, singing *God Save the Queen* and pledging to uphold the democratic values of the UK. It occurred to me that it was the second oath I had ever taken in my life. Some twenty years earlier I had given the Solemn Promise of the Pioneer, as did every nine- or ten-year-old in the Soviet Union. It went like this:

"I, Yana Bakunina...

...joining the ranks of the Soviet-wide pioneer organisation, named after Vladimir Ilyich Lenin

...in front of my comrades, solemnly promise

...to love and care for my motherland deeply

...to live, as bequeathed the Great Lenin

...as the Communist Party teaches

...and always abide by the laws of the pioneers of the Soviet Union."

At the time, it was the single most important event of my life, a moment of reverence shared by all my schoolmates with their scarlet neckerchiefs. We loved Lenin, and believed that "we will build our own, new world" ("*my nash, my novy mir postroim*"), but just a couple of years later we ditched the pioneer neckerchiefs and badges in shame. Impatient to get rid of the shackles that had chained the two generations before us, we ridiculed the oaths we had taken. In the twenty years that followed, we superimposed new values and ambitions onto our childhood memories, so that it became almost impossible to recall that cardinal point of our early world order.

Leaving the ceremonial chamber, I found myself pondering over my new status. It was not the oath or the test I had passed with flying colours that gave me a new passport, but ten years of perseverance. I had barely had a chance to take stock of my life, wiping tables, writing essays, crunching numbers, hand-holding clients and trying to fit in until finally I had earned a plum-covered booklet engraved with a lion and a unicorn. Inside I found a red grouse pecking at my face and forty-eight empty pages I was eager to fill up with travel stamps. It took me a few more years to realise that a British passport, along with an Oxford education and the City work experience, had opened more doors than just the ability to travel. I now had opportunities and freedoms my parents and grandparents could not have imagined.

At home I opened my Russian passport, which I had gratefully kept. The two passports lay cosily side by side while I planned my adventure, with Kamchatka just a dream away. If the British passport gave me freedom, the Russian one held my soul. My Russian roots gave me a mother tongue to read Pushkin's verse and filled my eyes with tears at the sound of Tchaikovsky. The word "*Ros-si-ya!*" chanted at international sport competitions always sends shivers down my spine and I cannot help but take every Russian victory or defeat extremely personally. Being Russian means making a wish on New Year's Eve, celebrating women on March 8th and insisting on an impromptu toast with every drink. My Russianness is my bluntness, but also my grit.

"You are one mad Russian!" exclaimed one managing

director when I told him I was leaving in the middle of the recession, while everyone else in the City was desperately clinging to their jobs. But then he wished me luck and said he would follow my shoestring adventures via my travel blog, because unlike me he was tied to his status, property and family commitments and would only ever consider sleeping in a tent for charity, an experience he would eagerly share at dinner parties for years to come.

***

Russia, summer 2009

I spent two months in Russia, travelling by train from the Baltic Sea to Vladivostok via the Urals and Siberia. My first stop was St. Petersburg, my favourite city in Russia, a treasure trove of history and culture.

St. Petersburg or *"Pieter"*, as the Russians like to call it, did not disappoint. The Nevsky Prospekt, the bridges over the Neva river, St. Isaac's Cathedral, the Winter Palace and the Palace Square were just as I remembered them, radiating in the glow of their imperial past. There was, however, a certain divider, casting its shadows throughout the city. Outside the historic centre, there sprouted ugly tower block neighbourhoods, completely devoid of greenery. "When developers bribe the city government, you can't expect to see public gardens", shrugged my friends. In the Russian Museum I found the familiar elderly ladies in old-fashioned suits, guarding the paintings of Vasnetsov, Surikov and Serov; by contrast, nearby Nevsky Prospekt and Sadovaya Street were dotted with exclusive designer shops filled with rich young customers. My friends bought me my beloved cheap and filling *kefir* for breakfast, then took me to expensive eateries, eager to impress me with the city's culinary scene, but I felt uneasy in my travelling clothes among the perfectly coiffed and made up clientele. St. Petersburg did not appear as money-crazed as Moscow or my native Ekaterinburg, but in fact it was two cities: one ruthlessly rich and one despondently poor.

It was on a train, covering three thousand kilometres from St. Petersburg to Ekaterinburg in thirty-six hours, that I finally met ordinary Russians. Of course, there was nothing ordinary about people travelling *platskart,* in the cheapest, communal, open-space carriage. There was an elderly woman returning home after a hip operation in St. Petersburg, who had somehow managed to climb up onto an upper bunk and stayed there, stoically enduring the journey. There was a young man from Bishkek watching the changing scenery as if it was a blockbuster movie. A Gazprom mechanic was heading north for his monthly shift at a gas transmission station where he wouldn't see anyone but a wandering reindeer shepherd for weeks at a time. A girl in her twenties was confused by the changing time zones, which affected her strict self-imposed rule not to eat after 6pm. She introduced herself as Masha, dressing her boiled egg and her pot of instant noodles with mayonnaise "Provençal", which was now sold in handy plastic pouches. We talked a little but the rhythmic rocking of the train soon cradled me to sleep. In the early hours, I was awoken by a ruckus at the other end of the carriage. Some pensioner had got drunk and spilled a can of gherkin brine onto a lady in ("brand new!") leopard pyjamas. She hit him with a *vobla* (a Caspian fish, usually consumed as a salt-dried beer snack), and the pair of them were reprimanded by Alla Vladimirovna, the carriage conductor. I could no longer sleep, anticipating my arrival home, and asked for some tea. Alla Vladimirovna served it to me in a glass with a traditional ornamented brass holder.

There was an almost unbearable heat wave in Ekaterinburg, with the air smelling of melting asphalt. My parents picked me up at the railway station and we passed through the city, which was much changed with new apartment buildings, gigantic shopping malls and roadside advertising stands, many of them empty. We drove to the *dacha*, where my parents now lived permanently. My father had added a smaller house next to the one built by my late grandfather. The original cottage too had been renovated and expanded, with a top floor to accommodate Baba Lena, auntie Natasha and uncle Borya, who came to stay in the country during the summer. The house now had proper plumbing and gas; upstairs my grandfather's hunting trophies were exhibited alongside family photographs, picked by auntie Natasha. She was now a proud grandmother, but her passion for cats lingered, as was evident from the pictures of an entire feline dynasty all called Basil. As soon as I arrived, auntie Natasha introduced me to Little Basil or *Vasilyek*, Russian for "cornflower", a shy kitten with fluffy blueish fur. Meanwhile, mum cooked a royal meal to welcome me home and we all sat down on the terrace and piled our plates high with marinated mushrooms, salads, *blinchiki* (pancakes filled with minced meat) and trout that my father had smoked himself. Baba Lena nudged uncle Borya to bring her some horseradish sauce, but he came back with her summer hat. Finally, once everyone's glasses were filled with Crimean sparkling wine, my father stood up to make a speech. He wasn't happy about me quitting my job and going travelling. Instead, he said, it was time for me to return to Russia and make myself useful to my Motherland. "You'll go on holiday when you turn fifty – now you must work", he said raising his glass.

I looked at my father, who had aged gracefully, with silver running through the hair on his temples. It merely added authority to his still young and handsome physiognomy. *Fathers and Sons*, a Turgenev novel which we had to read at school, came to mind not just as a catchy title but as an inevitable course served by life itself. My father's business, dependent on imports, had been shattered by the Russian financial crisis in 1998 and then dealt a fatal blow by the recession of 2008. He was forced to close down his firm after many agonising years navigating the choppy waters of lawlessness, bureaucracy, bribes and favours, all requisites of doing business in Russia. He, who had bravely embraced *perestroika* and the opportunities that came with it, had to admit failure, a common enough fate for any entrepreneur, but perhaps heart-breaking for a man brought up in the Soviet glory days. Now my father wanted me to make up for his own missed opportunities and get rich while I was young and able. For him, it seemed outright offensive that I was spending my savings on trotting around the globe with a backpack. For me, it was impossible to explain that after a decade of running on a treadmill, I simply needed a break.

We did not see eye to eye and soon I was whisked away by a fast train to Western Siberia. I had never been east of the Urals, and another train journey made me appreciate the vastness of my home country. We covered some 1,700km in 28 hours and arrived in Barnaul, the closest city to the Altai mountains, where Russia borders with China, Mongolia and Kazakhstan. Altai is a large area with emerald rivers, turquoise lakes, snow-capped peaks and glaciers, and it is crowned by mount Belukha, a double-headed 4,500m peak, the highest in Siberia. I booked a trek to the glacial Multa lakes and a rafting tour on the Katun river.

Trekking in Russia is an unforgettable experience. This is not least because there are few if any of the comforts now offered to casual hikers around the world, with food, tents and personal items carried by porters or mules. Before the trek our twenty-something guide Olya swiftly piled six tins of marrow "caviar", four rolls of ham, three loaves of bread, a kilo of buckwheat and a pack of biscuits – my share of the provisions – into my backpack. Over the course of five days we crossed meadows dotted with wild flowers, gushing streams and mountain passes. Olya expertly led the way despite there being no signs or obvious paths. In the evenings, we set up camp, gathered dry wood and made fire. Every dinner was a feast that Olya cooked from a handful of simple ingredients: chopped onions, carrots, grains and *tushonka,* tinned stewed meat – a Russian tourist staple. That first night we ate *plov* (pilaf), a Central Asian rice and meat dish, traditionally cooked in a cast iron pan. It was a simple, satisfying meal, which, after the long day, tasted like happiness. Our small group sat around the fire and shared a flask of vodka. Exhausted, we did not talk much. Something heavier than my backpack seemed to have been lifted from my shoulders.

One afternoon, after it had been raining, we stumbled upon a distinct footprint on a path, which could only belong to a bear. That evening we made a bigger fire and huddled closer together, staying up late. Olya made dessert from crumbled biscuits, walnuts, cacao and *sguschonka* (sweetened condensed milk), the best rocky road I'd ever tasted. We chatted about this and that and I mentioned my gay friends in London.

"The gays", suggested Lenar, "should be rounded up and burnt".

Lenar was a tourist from Kazan. His name was abbreviated from Lenin's Army. He was my age, worked in a bank, was married and had a toddler. The uninhibited brutality of his words shocked me.

"What are you saying?"

"Just that things got a bit loose – Stalin would've sorted them out", said Lenar and spat.

"You can't be serious…" I was stunned.

"Yana, you know it's not *normal*. Homosexuality isn't *natural*", said Alexey, another tourist.

I looked up. Alexey was a couple of years older than me. His pale skin, dark hair and handsome features made me think of Akunin's Erast Fandorin, a devastatingly romantic character. I had a crush on Alexey and would have swapped London for Novosibirsk, if he didn't have a girlfriend.

"I don't believe it… Who are you people? It's the twenty-first century!" I cried and ran to my tent.

There had been about ten of us sitting around the fire, yet no one had said a word. Those guys and girls were roughly my age, brought up at the same time as me. Sure, kids had called each other names like "lesbeyanka" (lesbian), which rhymed with my name "Yanka" and was used as an insult often enough. But then from the age of fifteen, I came across plenty of openly gay people in Ekaterinburg. It had never occurred to me to think of Russians as homophobic. Have people around me always thought of gays as "unnatural" or was it a more recent sentiment? I could forgive uneducated, narrow-minded people I'd never met, but Alexey...

I kept myself to myself the next day. In the evening, someone came up with yet another flask of vodka and raised a toast to "tolerance". I downed my shot. It was only later that I realised that the toast had called for *my* tolerance of Russian mores.

After days in the wilderness, we arrived at the Katun river for the rafting tour. I learned that rafting on a Siberian river wasn't all fun and recreation – it was an obstacle course. The water was freezing, and we were assured we'd last no more than twenty minutes if we capsized and were pulled away from the boat by the strong current. As if to demonstrate this, our rafting guide Andrey nearly drowned and once we got ashore, his numbness turned into an obscene stream of profanities, remarkable for a man of otherwise limited vocabulary.

Luckily, the camping site was by a village where, Andrey explained, there was a small grocery store selling a remedy for cold, shock and other maladies. Vodka was something mothers in Russia rubbed on the backs of their children to cure a chesty cough; a cloth soaked in vodka was often put on a forehead to reduce fever, and it was considered the best disinfectant for bites and cuts. We entered the village: a ramshackle scene of derelict houses, bent fences overgrown with shrubs and a large empty building without a roof. On it was a sign, barely legible, saying "School". Beside it there was a shop, or rather an opening in the wall of a residential house, with empty beer and vodka bottles on a windowsill.

"They don't sell much here", Andrey said "just booze and whatnot".

I bought a bottle of vodka to celebrate surviving the toughest section of Katun. It cost less than a bottle of water in the UK. Moments later, a man appeared from around the corner. He swayed as he walked towards us, carrying a three-litre glass can of honey. He stopped and, struggling to focus his eyes on me, said:

"Buy honey."

Altai honey has always been prized for its unique taste and medicinal properties. Wildflower or buckwheat honey sourced directly from Altai wasn't cheap.

"How much?" I asked out of pure curiosity. I was not going to take a three-litre can onto the raft, let alone around the world with me.

"Vodka," he mumbled, his eyes now fixed on the bottle I held.

"*Zapoy*" said Andrey quietly and turned to go. I followed him.

Zapoy (a drinking spree which lasts for days) wasn't something, I realised, I had ever come across before in my life. My years in Russia had been sheltered by growing up in an academic family, who lived relatively well even in the Soviet times. Sure my grandfather drank vodka, a couple of shots at dinner, a few more on bigger occasions. My parents drank beer and wine. I often got drunk with friends and suffered the next day. I had seen *zapoy* in films, with fictional characters on a bender for a week or two at a time. Yeltsin was said to fall off the wagon pretty frequently, embarrassing himself at home and abroad. Yet here I was walking through a ramshackle Russian village, neglected since the communist days, coming face to face with a ruined, pitiful and disgusting man.

"People here live from drink to drink," explained Andrey. "They make some money then guzzle it down, blaming the government and reminiscing about communism."

"Can't they get some livestock, start an organic farm?"

"Organic farm!" he laughed, "Russians would rather poison the neighbour's cow than bother with bettering their own lives."

We reached the bank and Andrey got busy making dinner. In the morning, just as we had packed and were about to set off again, the drunk appeared by the river. He looked wilder than the day before with a puffy red face and dishevelled hair. He came with a lamb, which pulled at a rope, trying to reach some grass to nibble on.

"Buy lamb... Vodka... Half a litre."

***

From Altai I travelled further east. My next stop was Baikal, the oldest and deepest freshwater lake in the world with an outstanding variety of endemic species, including *nerpa*, an endearing, pear-shaped Baikal seal. This largest reservoir of fresh water on the planet is growing by about two centimetres a year. The locals call it "the Sea". Buryats (indigenous people of Siberia, who share many traditions and customs with Mongols) worship it.

It was a Buryat family who gave me a lift from the ferry to Khuzir, the largest village on Olkhon, one of the two populated islands on Baikal. Olkhon is popular with tourists, who come here to relax on sandy beaches, sample *omul*, a very tasty endemic fish, and perhaps even meet a shaman. Foreign tourists aren't too popular with the local trade: "They take pictures of *omul* and ask for tinned tuna." The Buryat family stopped by a roadside pile of rocks, decorated with bright ribbons, to pay their respects to the spirits of the island. The custom involved pouring some vodka over the stones and … drinking the rest. It wasn't yet noon, but "when in Rome, do as Romans do."

The Buryats showed me Cape Burkhan, a sacred rock shaped like a sail, surrounded by clear, cool water. They also recommended the best place for *saguday* (raw *omul*, diced and served with chopped onions and spices), smoked *omul* and *pozy*, the Buryat national dish – large meat dumplings closely resembling Tibetan *momos*. I found a place for the night and stayed up late watching the sun setting over Baikal. It took its time, then just after ten at night it sank, with a thick, dark curtain promptly drawing over the horizon.

It was still dawn when I heard some commotion in the yard of my guesthouse. It sounded like an army unit was being woken up for its morning drill. I wasn't far off: a club of young boxers from Irkutsk had come to Olkhon for their summer training camp. The boxers were between ten and sixteen years old. Their head coach liked to sleep in after "a few too many" the night before, so it fell to the assistant coach to take the lads out first thing. Curious, I joined them. We ran to the beach to find Baikal covered with a fluffy, white duvet. Catching my breath, I took a good look at Russia's future Olympic talent. They looked lean and strong but their feet made my heart sink. Only a couple of them had proper sneakers on – the rest wore slippers, flip flops, sandals or old sports shoes which barely held together. They trained diligently that morning and again after breakfast when their head coach emerged, red-faced and vicious, until he was soothed by a bottle of beer and some dried *omul*, fetched by his quick-witted assistant.

***

"Kam-chat-ka." I leant closer to the aeroplane window to see if I could spot active volcanoes or the famous Avacha creek, where the Russians had defeated the French and the British fleet in 1854 during the Crimean War. A mean cloud denied me, but minutes later the plane landed in Petropavlovsk-Kamchatsky. After the maddening four-day train journey from Irkutsk to Vladivostok and a three-hour flight, I was finally in the land I had daydreamed about back in my maroon-walled cubicle in the City of London.

I headed straight for the market to buy some fresh salmon caviar. There were plenty of seafood stalls, each laden with fresh, smoked and dried fish and gigantic jars of caviar. Succulent coral-red roe belonged to *gorbusha, keta, nerka, semga, chavyucha* and *losos'*, humbly translated into English as "salmon". The trade was slow, they said, with Kamchatka, an expensive destination, enjoying but a modest flow of tourists because of the recession. I bought some of the most prized *chavycha* caviar, handed to me in a plastic container. I ate it by the stall using a crab claw as a spoon, which must have been a wild spectacle for the locals.

Over the next ten days I explored Kamchatka, climbing fuming volcanoes, freezing in the snowstorm, then soaking myself back to life in thermal pools. I went rafting down a slow river Bystraya (ironically called "fast") and explored craters of extinguished volcanoes with surreally turquoise lakes inside. It did not take long for the land of vapour jets, sulphur whirlpools, lava rocks and spectacular mountain vistas to pierce my heart. Just like the summit of an active volcano, gurgling, spitting and breaking into hot tears, I felt alive, bursting with joy and crying from happiness. I had been surrounded by people, who just like me, were possessed by wanderlust. After one particularly memorable day (featuring a FSB colonel sliding down a snow-covered slope on his backside, yodelling with joy) we sat around the fire – a cancer surgeon from Moscow, a corporate lawyer from St. Petersburg, a FSB colonel from Ekaterinburg and me – and drank *nastoyka* (vodka flavoured with herbs; in Kamchatka they made *nastoyka* with sliced garlic and a local herb called *puchka*), grateful to call Russia our homeland.

On another day we made camp by the river. While the tourists drenched themselves in mosquito repellent, our guides caught some *forel'*, *harius* and *golets* (trout) and made *ukha*, a traditional Russian fish soup. I learned that the broth ought to be made with smaller, less valuable fish, which are discarded before the "stars of the catch" are added to the pot. As a final touch, a shot of vodka is poured into the soup for that extra oomph. When someone asked me about my plans for after travelling, I was much more interested in writing down the *ukha* recipe.

On the day of my departure from Kamchatka (and Russia), my flight was cancelled because of a storm, and I spent the night in a lifeless hotel room by the airport. In tune with the skies, I broke down and wept. A certain local guide with captivating green eyes and a radiant smile had prompted the downpour. I had become fond of his company and was sorry to be leaving. But my emotions were more complicated than that. It was Kamchatka that had hooked me; it was Russia that had got under my skin. I could not have predicted that I'd feel so much at ease crammed in *platzkart* or hiking in the wilderness. The sheer scale of Russia was quite impossible to take in, and I felt overwhelmed by its many fascinating nooks to which I could travel in the future. But it was the Russians I met – open, hospitable and generous – who touched me most. They made me feel loved and welcomed. I sobbed like the Angara, the only river flowing out of Baikal, unable to change its course and certain only of the journey itself, but not of its ultimate purpose.

Chapter XIII in which I got to say "I work in TV"

By the end of 2009, the price of oil had begun to rise again, and the Russian economy was back on its feet. However, the recession years had exposed the vulnerability of the country's primitive economic model. Pensioners, who relied on state support, had struggled. The middle classes, who had become used to the Western consumer lifestyle, had been hit by mass redundancies. Staying out of politics no longer kept bellies full.

Meanwhile, Putin, who had already served two consecutive terms as president, appointed himself as prime minister and installed a diminutive sidekick, Dmitry Medvedev, as Russia's president. Medvedev talked about liberalism and modernisation. He recorded video blogs and posted on social media. However, little changed, and soon Putin announced that he would be returning to the presidency. In December 2011, reports of parliamentary electoral fraud and discontent with the government kleptocracy sent tens of thousands of pensioners, students and the middle classes onto the streets of Moscow. It was the largest public protest since 1991. Putin's popularity ratings began to slide.

The Kremlin reacted by switching on the propaganda machine. This time it was loaded with ideology, something Russian people were used to from the Soviet days. The new rhetoric preached Russia's unique path: orthodoxy, national integrity and collective psyche. It identified a common enemy – the West. Anything falling outside traditional values – homosexuals, liberals, punks who dared to protest against Putin in a church – were labelled evil. The message was consistently spread across all media.

London, 2010-2013

I am often asked if I would move back to Russia. I used to say that my corporate finance background would only be suitable for a job in Moscow, a city I had never loved. For me, Moscow meant exasperating traffic jams and sour-faced people, who spoke with a mildly irritating, chichi accent and looked down on provincial folks like me. In Moscow, but also in Ekaterinburg, people appeared to be obsessed with status and money. Everyone was a "manager" of some kind, regardless of whether or not they were supervising a team. Even a hygienist at a dental practice was called "manager of mouth hygiene". It was imperative to have the best car you could (or could not) afford, an *inomarka*, of course. Designer clothes, Swiss watches, newly-built flats and mistresses were the common measure of happiness. My childhood friend Anya once asked me why I wasn't wearing designer jeans, while brazenly checking the label at the back of my top. Another former classmate, who worked for a large US corporation in Moscow, told me a story about wearing a *short* mink coat to a corporate event. She had been looked down upon, and had felt ashamed for years afterwards.

After I became disillusioned with banking, I sought career advice from a successful Russian businessman. He said: "If you want to get rich, come to Moscow. You'll find a job in an instant. Unless it's not what you want?" I looked at him sitting in his elegant office, with holiday photos from his house in the Alps and a private island in the Maldives, and I shook my head. His question made me think. At my happiest, I was jumping on a plane with a book in my hand, heading to a new destination, perhaps to climb Mont Blanc or Kilimanjaro or to explore a new city. I loved being outdoors. I had become an avid runner and was often found in Hyde Park crawling in the mud, as part of the military-style fitness regime which had become popular in London. Instead of dining out all the time, I began to cook and loved having friends round for dinner. It was true that during my travels in Russia I had found many like-minded people, but I sensed that the corporate environment in Moscow, Ekaterinburg or Novosibirsk would feel rather different from the blue skies of Kamchatka. In short, I chose to love Russia from afar.

Over the years the distance I felt from Russia grew from a crack into an abyss. It was a question of values, and mine have changed.

***

In summer 2010, after a year of travelling, I returned to London and began looking for a job. My former boss recommended me to a couple of TV production groups, and one of them had a vacancy at their headquarters. I got a job at a company called Zodiak Media, which had been formed by the merger of two European TV production groups. I was quickly absorbed in learning how to make money in TV and how to manage a group of forty companies spread across twenty countries. My work still focussed on spreadsheets, but I also mingled with creative people, who fascinated me. I felt like an anthropologist who had discovered a new species after a lifetime spent among Economics & Management students and investment bankers.

My new office environment could not have been more different from the finance one. We usually began the day discussing the previous night's TV shows; we'd watch show reels and try to work out what made *My Big Fat Gypsy Wedding* such a hit. We'd laugh all the time, invent elaborate nicknames for senior executives, pull pranks and go out for lunch on Fridays. Work was fun. I stopped wearing power suits and adopted a more casual dress sense. Every October I'd find myself on a yacht in Cannes, drinking champagne on the deck to celebrate the annual international TV programme market. I loved saying "I work in TV", especially when I did not have to explain that I was just a corporate mole, basking in the glamour associated with working in the media.

Of course, it wasn't all fun and games. Part of my remit was to look after the Russian TV production companies within the group. They were managed by an enigmatic man who looked like a villain from a James Bond movie. He also wore a suffocating eau de cologne. Early on I was sent to meet him in Moscow to learn about his projects and challenges and report back to HQ. General Grubozaboyschikov (*From Russia with Love* – I won't use his real name) invited me for dinner at a nice restaurant, where, like many of Russia's rich, he was obnoxious to the waiters but very attentive to me. Afterwards we walked back to my hotel, its lobby busy with high-class hookers looking for prey. We sat down by the bar and the General lit a cigarette. He chain-smoked the entire pack while he told me about the business. I learned about the

213

mafia 'offering' to protect the business for a monthly fee and the police promising not to hassle them for a similarly healthy retainer. There were tax police bombarding the company with surprise visits, bound to find an 'irregularity' until its manager gave in and agreed to pay up. There were commissioning broadcasters with various ideas about personal kickbacks depending on the importance of the channel. At the top of the hierarchy sat Konstantin Ernst, the tsar of Channel One, who has been the Kremlin's Master of Ceremonies at Russia's dominant state channel since 1999.

I could not believe it. Corruption was reported in the media and was the subject of edgy television series. It wasn't something I ever expected to come across directly. Yet there I was, sitting in the lobby of a Moscow hotel, feeling sick from the smoke and the stories I was being told by the General who, apart from the nearly empty pack of cigarettes, looked remarkably composed. It was as if he was telling me about the new detective series in the pipeline. At the end he laughed – a sinister sound effect coming from the depths of his formidable gut – and asked me: "So what are you going to tell your boss?"

I returned to London and over the weekend binged on *Glukhar*, a Russian crime series about two childhood friends, one working as a detective and the other as a traffic policeman in one of Moscow's neighbourhoods. They bend the law, abuse their power, take bribes from the rich but often help people in need. *Glukhar*, the main character, a sort of Russian Robin Hood, is sleeping with his boss; his friend is dating a prostitute. The series, written as an observation of the typical day-to-day life of two policemen, was first broadcast in Russia in 2008 and became extremely popular. My mum never missed any of its one hundred and sixty episodes, enamoured of the main character.

Watching the series helped me calm down, and it became very clear to me that with my Oxford education and my London work experience, I'd be hopeless in Russia. In Britain, I relied on supply and demand, profit and loss, merit and hard work. I lived in a world sheltered by the guiding principles of law, ethics and economics. In the chambers of Westminster, Members of Parliament squabbled over expenses, the "mansion tax" and flexible working policy, which to me were all signs of a healthy democracy. It implied that the big issues had broadly been addressed. In the meantime, the Russian parliament approved the bill extending the presidential term from four years to six. Similar measures were adopted in local government institutions, effectively supporting the lawlessness of the incumbents in power. In Russia, it seemed, people adapted to the style of business, where bribes, favours and paybacks were routine. They conformed and survived. I, on the other hand, had got used to living in the greenhouse of the Western world and would surely wilt and perish in the harsh Russian reality.

I told my boss what he expected to hear: Russia was "hairy" but the General was a resourceful man, used to the specifics of doing business there. His division brought in revenue and healthy profits. It would be best to leave him to his own devices and focus on underperforming managers elsewhere. And that's what we did.

***

It was in summer 2012 when something unexpected happened to me. I was at a concert of the Icelandic band Of Monsters and Men with my university friend, Fiona. She told me about her idea of launching a women's magazine, which would be intelligent like *The Economist* and cover everything from current affairs to career advice, cooking, parenting and culture. She thought there was a gap in the market, with women's periodicals dominated by gossip and fashion. I was not sure about print as a viable business model and told her so, but I liked the idea of focussing on smart and discerning women, who could do with some inspiration. At work I was beginning to get bored of the endless number-crunching, so perhaps I too was looking for something new to stimulate my personal development. It was at that concert that I came up with an idea of organising an event where I would interview three inspirational women from different professional backgrounds in front of a live female audience. I'd help them tell their stories and encourage other women to explore their talents. I called it *Ladies Who Impress*.

Over the next few days, whether I was running on Hampstead Heath in the mornings or cycling to and from work, I was thinking about my event. I had never organised anything like it, I hadn't done much public speaking, let alone interviewed anyone. It was the summer of the London Olympics, when spectator sports took over the city. The atmosphere filled me with inspiration and fearlessness, as if anything was possible. I found two heroines for my first event, Sarah Hyndman, a creative entrepreneur, and Hanna Sykulska-Lawrence, a space scientist who had designed microscopic equipment for the 2008 NASA mission to Mars and was the youngest British engineer on the team at just twenty-six. I was looking for one more star for the night and I soon found her.

I went to see *The Curious Incident of the Dog in the Night-Time*, a brilliant National Theatre production based on the novel by Mark Haddon. The play was directed by Marianne Elliott, an exceptionally talented woman who had previously earned critical acclaim for her production of *War Horse*. After I left the theatre, deeply moved by the play, I knew that I had to find Marianne and persuade her to help me. A couple of days later I was back at the theatre, this time listening to a live interview with Marianne about her production. She talked to a journalist from the *Observer*. An impudent thought crossed my mind: *I could do the interview just as well, if not better.* It was a warm night and I felt like lingering at the Southbank for a little longer. As I walked from the Cottesloe Theatre to the river, I saw Marianne talking to someone by the stage door. It was my chance! I made my plea and she must have seen something in my eyes, which now shone with excitement every time I talked about *Ladies Who Impress*, because she said: "Why don't you write down your idea and leave a note for me with your contact details at the stage door?"

"Handwritten?"

"Yes," and she was off.

There was something very special about that idea because my thoughts and hopes were soon pirouetting together on two pages of a Moleskin notebook, like a troupe of impassioned amateurs. Marianne said yes and at the end of September I sent out emails to all London-based women I knew, inviting them to a *Ladies Who Impress* charity event. One friend helped me book a prestigious venue, another paid for it. One colleague built me a simple website, another put together a playlist. It helped that I was raising money for the Huntington's Disease Association. Some seventy women bought tickets and came to Soho's Groucho Club to support me and celebrate *Ladies Who Impress*.

The room was crammed with women who, I was pleased to see, had dressed up for the occasion. I used bar stools as an improvised stage but I had not thought of organising chairs for the spectators. I welcomed the audience, promising them inspiring stories of ordinary women who had achieved extraordinary success. I then began my first interview with Sarah Hyndman, who was visibly nervous. Her voice trembled as she began to answer my first question. And then something wonderful happened. The spectators, as if on cue, sat down on the floor. Marianne was among them, settled in the front row. That gesture of support immediately filled Sarah with confidence. She relaxed and became engaging, just like when we had practised. I looked at the women in front of us and realised I knew only about a third of the audience. These women were friends of friends who had come because they were genuinely interested, not as a favour to me. I read it in their eyes.

I interviewed Marianne next and noticed that I felt completely at ease. The previous couple of months had been a frenzy of preparation and nerves, but there I was finally enjoying myself on the night. It was an out-of-body experience; I was fully engaged with Marianne, as she spoke about dreading every single opening night, regardless of her years of experience, and at the same time I was thinking:

There is something in this, "Yana, the broadcaster..." I may even have found myself. After the interviews, most guests stayed on, to the delight of the Groucho Club staff behind the bar. I was basking in congratulations and words of support. There was something else a friend picked up on. She said that my event was so unlike a typical City networking evening with women in power suits competing to impress each other. Indeed, I had wanted to showcase role models from diverse backgrounds, and in my audience too there were lawyers and writers, yoga teachers and academics, single women and married mothers. At the end of the night I encouraged everyone to think of their own "mission impossible", something suitably audacious, but not unachievable. I knocked down another glass of champagne, took a bright pink post-it note and printed: "WRITE AND PUBLISH A BOOK."

***

A couple of weeks later I was having dinner with my friends Urvi and Anand. I told them about *Ladies Who Impress*; I was so excited I hardly touched my food. We were sitting in the basement of a tiny restaurant in Soho; it was packed, and the pungent smell from the kitchen travelled into the dining room.

"What are you going to do?" Anand asked me, refilling our glasses. Later he admitted, not without a touch of envy, that he'd never seen me or anyone else so exhilarated about a new project.

"Give me until the end of June next year and then you'll see," I replied. I didn't have a plan or even an inkling, I was probably a little intoxicated, but I knew that my life had taken a new turn and I had no choice but to follow it.

"All right then. If you leave your job, I'll give up bread for a month," said Anand, mopping up a plate of curry with a fluffy piece of naan bread. His wife looked at him in astonishment.

"You're on," I said shaking his hand. There was nothing I liked more than a challenge.

In truth, I forgot all about the wager. In the first few months of 2013, my life became a hotpot, filled to the brim with work, new ideas and anguished soul-searching. Everything was happening at a hundred miles an hour, with my mind racing ahead of my bike, which took me from my home in north London to the office in West Kensington and back. Work became incredibly busy, with the company's management arguing with its main shareholder over strategy. New projects kept landing on my plate, and I was churning out increasingly complicated spreadsheets and travelling to Stockholm, Paris, Milan and Los Angeles for meetings. All the while my mind never stopped grinding over new ideas, obsessed by my new creative endeavour. In L.A. I would stay up building a model until late at night, but in the morning I'd be running along Santa Monica beach and thinking of a new theme for my next celebration. I organised two more *Ladies Who Impress* events and even interviewed the London Olympics legend Katherine Grainger, who had won Gold in the women's double sculls. Creative work became the umami flavour of my life, but my inspirational networking events weren't a sustainable business. Was it just a hobby? Could I take it further? *How?* Those questions kept simmering away day and night.

On the one hand, I felt inspired by the women I had interviewed to take a leap of faith and strike out on my own. Jenny Dawson, a social entrepreneur who had started a business of making chutneys from fruit and vegetables discarded at New Covent Garden Market, London's wholesale market, in order to tackle food waste, talked to me about her naiveté. She said that in hindsight she might not have knocked on the doors of Selfridges, Fortnum & Mason and other prestigious food department stores; she would not have involved disadvantaged women before she had established herself better and found a proper professional kitchen; she would probably not have quit her job at a hedge fund so early on. Yet precisely because she was naive and so driven by her idea, she had done all those things and succeeded. Jenny and other women I had spoken to were so different from the women I had encountered in the City at the beginning of my career, when I could have done with more guidance and support. Instead of role models I could relate to, I came across women who were either intimidating or pitiful. None inspired me. Now I met women who seemed ordinary in the sense that they had the same doubts, prejudices and fears as me, and yet they opened restaurants, published books, won Olympic medals. It was contagious.

On the other hand, without a viable business plan it felt mad to give up my secure life. I had a well-paid job. My respectable role in a large, multinational business gave me a certain status. I could afford to dine out, go to the theatre in the West End, fly to Venezuela, Jordan and Iceland to feed my travel bug. Friends who still worked in banking sought me out for advice on how to move from the City into corporate roles. To all appearances, I led a pleasant, comfortable life. It ticked boxes. I should have been happy.

I wasn't. My mind, the hotpot of ideas, internal struggles, aspirations and dreams, reached a boiling point. I quit my job. June 30th 2013 was my last day in the office. I walked out in a daze, but I never looked back. My friend Anand said "Unbelievable!" and begrudgingly went on a diet.

Some time later I had drinks with the company's outgoing chief executive, David Frank. David, an entrepreneur at heart, had also left the business to start a new venture after he had realised that being a captain of a gigantic cruise ship was nowhere near as exciting as braving the ocean in a dingy. It was a hot day and we sat outside. David wasn't my direct boss and previously I'd only spoken to him in private a handful of times, but I respected him hugely. If he had told me then that I was barking mad, that I should beg for my job back or find another one, I would probably have done just that. Instead, he asked me about my plans and listened to me patiently. I said I wanted to try things out: organise more *Ladies Who Impress* events, perhaps launch talks and workshops to help inspire people, not just women, to uncover their talents; and to start a blog. It must have sounded like a right mess, but David, who usually said everything with a smile, looked at me seriously and said: "Go for it. You can't ever predict if things will work out but what you *can* do is do your best."

Chapter XIV in which I became a journalist

A crisis in Ukraine, when peaceful demonstrations against the president Victor Yanukovich turned bloody in February 2014, rang alarm bells for the Kremlin. Putin could not allow the dissident fire to spread to Russia. At the same time the situation in Kiev presented an opportunity to stage a primetime drama. The Russian national TV channels dedicated most of their air time to the crisis in Ukraine, condemning the pro-EU sentiment in Kiev and the newly elected government led by Petro Poroshenko. The US and the West were assigned the roles of villains, stirring trouble at the Russian doorstep.

The state-owned networks portrayed the separatists fighting for the independence of the Donbass area of Ukraine as the righteous underdogs. By contrast, Ukrainian government forces were branded as neo-Nazis, who were raping and looting the Russian-speaking population of Eastern Ukraine. The Russian media showed fake footage and even used actors. Meanwhile, liberal TV channels and internet sites in Russia were shut down, while pro-Kremlin trolls viciously attacked any government critics.

In March 2014, after an unconstitutional referendum, the Crimea, the Ukrainian peninsula (strategically important for Russia due its proximity to the Russian naval base on the Black Sea) became a federal subject of Russia. The mainstream media played on the people's nostalgia for the glorious days of the Soviet Union and trumpeted the news "Crimea is ours!" Only 3% of Russians disapproved of the annexation. Putin's popularity, as measured by polls, went up to nearly 90%.

Paris, February 2015

Paris has a habit of disappointing romantically inclined visitors with bouts of inclement weather. My cheap umbrella was useless against the mischievous rain, which came at me sideways, but fortunately I soon spotted the café I was looking for. Inside it was almost empty, but somehow, even with just a few patrons the café had a pleasant ambience, with faded green walls, books on windowsills and a tray of croissants on the counter. I was early and ordered a coffee.

I recognised him immediately: Simon Kuper looked exactly like his profile picture on the first page of the *FT Weekend* magazine. A week earlier I had been in touch with him on a whim and asked for advice. I was contemplating applying for an internship at the *Financial Times* and wondered if I needed a degree in journalism to write features. It was an opportunistic email to a Paris-based columnist whose no-nonsense writing I admired. I was going to Paris to visit a friend and thought I'd try my luck. Simon agreed to meet me and surprised me again by ordering tea. In my mind, journalists lived on black coffee, and famous columnists were too important to waste their time on amateur bloggers like me.

I had had a go at a few different projects since quitting my job and come to realise that writing was "my thing". I held five more *Ladies Who Impress* events, which were increasingly difficult to pull off. My one-person outfit was competing with the marketing power of *Stylist*, *Grazia* and *Red* magazines, who were also organising networking events for women. I began interviewing women in private and publishing their stories on my website. Over a couple of years, I have interviewed ninety women and built up a healthy readership. I launched inspirational talks and workshops, but discovered that the London marketplace was already pretty crowded. On the other hand, my blog *Life Tonic*, with 'shots' of inspiration on personal development, entrepreneurship, economics and life skills became modestly popular. I wrote two posts a week for the *Ladies Who Impress* and *Life Tonic* websites. Once I gave myself permission to write, it was just a matter of committing time and sticking to it. Writing, I discovered, might sprout from talent but it would only flourish with discipline.

"Don't worry about a degree, find yourself a niche and start building a portfolio of articles," said Simon. "You know about finance – could that be your angle? What about Russia?"

"Yes, Russia," I agreed. Since the Maidan revolution in Ukraine, I felt it had become impossible to stay out of politics. I told Simon about my close friend Anya and her husband, both supporting Putin and his Crimean manoeuvre.

They argued that Crimea was a piece of the puzzle which had belonged to Russia historically, and that Putin was a hero for returning it. It is true that the Crimean Peninsula had been part of the Russian Empire since 1783 when the Turkish Ottoman and Catherine the Great had first agreed on its independence and later Russia had annexed it. Crimea was a district within the Russian Soviet Socialist Republic when the Soviet Union had been formed in 1921. When Nikita Khrushchev had given Crimea to Ukraine in 1954 as a gesture of friendship, it didn't matter because it was still part of the USSR. But in 1991 when Ukraine had declared its independence, Russia "lost" its favourite vacation spot, and its Black Sea fleet stationed at the Crimean Peninsula became vulnerable. Most Crimean people are ethnically Russian and would have benefitted from closer ties to Russia, rather than economically weaker Ukraine. This much I sympathised with. I also believed that if Crimea had been given a democratic, lawful choice, it would have voted to reunite with Russia. But that was not what had happened. As a result, Anya, her husband and I quarrelled bitterly in the previously amicable atmosphere of their kitchen.

Simon and I talked for about an hour – I could hardly believe it. He explained that once upon a time he too had benefited from someone else's generosity early in his career. I felt inspired and very grateful for his time and advice. As I hurried back to my friend's flat, my mind was already working on my first article. I didn't worry about my lack of experience or the competitiveness of freelance writing. I owed it to Simon to get it right and have my piece published. A week later my article, 'Vladimir Putin has torn my family apart', appeared in the online edition of the *New Statesman*.

***

London, 2015 – 2016

Since moving to Britain, I had barely followed current affairs in Russia. At first I had felt annoyed at the predictably antagonistic coverage of Russian politics by such outlets as *The Times*. For example, I remember how the broadsheet accused Russia of injustice when it had raised the price of gas it was selling to Ukraine in order to bring it closer to the real market value. But I found I was more interested in fiction than news. I devoured a history of ancient Rome, Italian crime and science fiction with equally ravenous appetites. My father scolded me for not taking enough interest in my Motherland, but after office hours I preferred switching off the screens and not spending my time browsing Russian-language websites. When, in 2013, I set up on my own, my quest for fulfilment and the freelance corporate finance consulting work I took on to support myself and my creative projects consumed all my energy. But the events in Ukraine, which had begun with a peaceful protest against government corruption on Maidan Nezalezhnosti, Kiev's Independence Square, in November 2013, and had led to riots, political crisis, civil war in Donbass and Russia's annexation of Crimea, changed everything. The Russian and Western media outlets painted vastly different pictures of what was happening. My Russian friends on social media talked about Ukrainians with a hatred I could not understand. My own father sent me an email entitled "Crimea is ours! And are *you* ours?"

I was not an expert on Russia, I could not provide sound political analysis, but I could write about my personal experience of becoming estranged from my family and finding myself a world apart from many of my Russian friends. My first article was the most painful one, but like an unbearably high pile of dirty dishes, it had to be dealt with. My father was convinced I had been brainwashed by Western propaganda; he called me a disappointment because I wasn't a patriot. A patriot in his eyes was a person who lived in Russia and supported Putin the Saviour in his struggle against the evils of the West. In some of the more heated debates we had at home, he called me a "national traitor", a member of the "fifth column". My father, who had turned sixty, was talking about volunteering in Donbass, fighting for the pro-Russian separatists. He ranted about Western NGOs in Russia being CIA agents and supported the Kremlin's ban on them. Mercifully, my mother and I agreed not to talk about politics, thereby preserving our relationship.

How is it that my intelligent, inquisitive, rebellious father has become what I can hardly bring myself to commit to paper – a Putin lover? I wanted to understand it, examine my own sentiment and organise my thoughts into logical compartments. My parents watched the news every morning and every night. I was convinced that it was the relentless Kremlin propaganda that had distorted reality, encouraged hatred and cultivated the lowest instincts in people, even in my parents. Television, the dominant Russian media, destroyed judgement and intelligence. I watched popular talk shows where the words "homosexual" and "paedophile" were used interchangeably. I watched the news bulletins which followed exactly the same script every day: Putin the Wise signs a decree in his royal office, Putin the Brave visits a far province, while the USA, the corrupt state, messed up by so-called democratic values, is suffering another natural disaster, a terrorist attack or a mass shooting in a public place. Orwell's two minutes of hate were skilfully extrapolated by the spin doctors at Russia's Channel One. I had no doubt that Western media too were guilty of biased reporting, but the scale and the intensity of the Kremlin propaganda was unrivalled.

Could Newspeak be so strong and effective by itself? It was not until I read *The Invention of Russia* by Arkady Ostrovsky that I understood that propaganda fed not so much on ignorance but on resentment. Russian people, even the most brilliant entrepreneurs, were ultimately helpless against the vulnerability of Russia's undeveloped economy, extortionate bank loan rates, the ubiquitous corruption and bureaucracy. Any hopes they had harboured in the early *perestroika* days now seemed naive. However, unmet personal ambitions were alleviated by the growing strength and importance of the Russian state. The annexation of Crimea gave people a sense of victory and pride. Being part of the bigger and stronger Russia – a patriotic image concocted by the media – compensated for personal failures and disappointments in life.

I sent my first article to Simon Kuper and he replied, "You can write." Inspired, I pressed on. I spoke to ordinary people in Moscow, Kiev and Ekaterinburg, as well as Russian expatriates living in London. I developed stories which were important to me, untangling the questions I pondered over myself. I wrote about Putin's popularity, deciphering his 86% approval rating in February 2015. People I interviewed liked his strong image, his shrewdness, his commitment to restoring Russia's might. Russians supported Putin, even called him *batyushka* (the holy father), because they had regained national self-respect and arisen from the financial ashes of the 1990s. Putin brought back stability. Individual freedoms and democracy seemed empty words in comparison to the collective sense of status and integrity, reminiscent of the Soviet superpower days. "Russia needs an authoritarian leader, a disciplinarian," I was told, "Russians cannot be ruled with a carrot, we understand only the stick."

In May 2014, one of the opposition leaders in Russia, Boris Nemtsov, criticised the Kremlin propaganda, saying "people are set off against each other. This hell cannot end peacefully." He was shot dead in February 2015 in the centre of Moscow. Western media and their readers were outraged. Most Russians just laughed. The independent, opposition-friendly Moscow-based radio station Echo of Moscow broadcast interviews with Nemtsov, and history books remembered him as a one-time primary candidate to succeed Yeltsin, but the mainstream media had pushed him to the margin, like a piece of debris. In comparison to Putin's rating, Boris Nemtsov was no more important than an average citizen. What troubled me most was that Russian people hadn't been perturbed by the murder; life was business as usual and the important thing was to stay out of politics.

Later that year I watched *Leviathan*, a Russian film which had received many accolades in the West since its release at Cannes, but wasn't shown in Russia until 2015. Andrey Zvyagintsev directs a compelling drama, set in a remote northern backwater on the Barents Sea. The story is a documentary of Russian life, drenched in vodka and despair, pickled with the corruption of the church and peppered with violent crime. At the end of the film there is a reference to the biblical trial of Job, who was advised to accept his fate – or else. I remember feeling numb. The film was partly financed by the Russian Ministry of Culture, which was astounding. It's as if the State had funded the film's message: "Yes, we can squash a person like a louse, and if you ever dare say a word against the system, we'll destroy your life too."

I could not blame Russian people for staying out of politics, but I was shocked to discover that some had forgotten the lessons from our history. In May 2015, I flew to Moscow for an article about the Victory Day celebrations. I watched the grandiose military parade on television, which unsettled me, then joined a commemorative march on Tverskaya Street. It was an unusually hot day, yet hundreds of thousands of people, including the elderly and young children, walked towards Red Square, carrying enlarged black-and-white photographs of the Great Patriotic War veterans. The so-called "Immortal Regiment" march, now held annually on May 9th in many Russian cities and abroad, wasn't masterminded in the Kremlin: the idea had been born in Tomsk in 2012, where a couple of journalists had come up with the plan to commemorate local veterans by carrying their photos on the Victory Day. I was genuinely moved by the atmosphere in Moscow, where the air was thick with gratitude, pride and contemplation. And then I saw the face of Stalin.

A young woman was carrying a large crimson flag with his unmistakeable image. The innocent wind tickled the fabric. Then I spotted an older man marching with a poster of Stalin, which depicted the Leader dressed in military uniform and adorned with medals. I was stunned. A few months later I was back in Moscow to face the fact that the fleeting image of Stalin, had, like a cancerous cell, spread everywhere. At the busy Moscow Domodedovo airport, there were souvenir mugs and badges featuring a man with a moustache, coiffed hair and unsmiling eyes. Men wearing Stalin t-shirts walked the streets of Moscow, and calendars with the twelve photos of the "Red Tsar" were spread across the counters of the bookshops. New statues of Stalin appeared in some cities, commissioned and erected by Russia's Communist Party. Charles de Gaulle, the former French president, had been right: "Stalin didn't walk away into the past, he dissolved into the future."

Stalin's positive image in Russia today is cultivated mostly through his association with the Great Patriotic War. "Stalin saved us from the Nazis," people say. It is inconvenient to remember that it was Stalin who had signed a non-aggression pact with Hitler in August 1939 and had been falsely assured that Germany would not invade the Soviet Union. Stalin disregarded several reports from his own intelligence agents and defected German spies about the advance of Hitler's army in 1941. Millions of lives were lost as a result when the Germans did invade. But the cancer is spreading beyond the interpretation of history. The positive opinion of Stalin seems to be a reflection of Russian society's demand for order and national safety. People conjure the image of Stalin as the strict, imperious and powerful father. *Batya, batyushka* (old Russian: father, holy father) …

My article about Stalin was translated into Russian and published on a popular website which collates select foreign press articles on Russia. A friend spotted it for me. The translation was fair, and I was just about to close my laptop when I saw the comments under the article. The comments section had been open for just forty-eight hours after publication, but plenty of people had taken the time to add their opinions, some of them longer than the article itself. There were about a hundred comments, some prompting further discussion among the readers. A few people agreed with my horror at seeing Stalin back, but most zealots found a dozen ways to stamp on my article and me, sparing no graphic details of the execution I apparently deserved. I read every single comment, transfixed. If I was an experienced journalist, I'd pull myself away, I'd laugh at the pseudo-intellectuals, I'd even consider my work a success for attracting so much attention. Alas, that day I only saw an appalling bottomless pit.

Later I was told that the Kremlin bank-rolled internet trolls. While I didn't agree with most Russians about Putin and his politics, I found enough like-minded people among my network of Russian family and friends to give me optimism. Not everyone bought the lies they were fed on television and felt content with Putin's kleptocracy. It also helped that for me, writing about Russia was only a hobby. I dipped in and out, I put myself in Russian shoes for no longer than a week at a time. I wasn't my cousin, who had lost his job as soon as the Russian economy fell into recession or his son, a student, fretting about the change in conscription laws which could mean being sent to a war zone. I wasn't my former English teacher, Elena Aleksandrovna, whose pension now barely covered rent, food and medicine. I wasn't my friend who worked as a broadcaster in Moscow and had to learn to censor himself to keep his job and his comfortable lifestyle. I didn't have to be careful about "popularising homosexuality … including instilling distorted ideas that society places an equal value on traditional and non-traditional sexual relations". I was safely tucked away in London, writing my blogs, travelling and making a living from consulting. My version of Russia and my hopes for it were nurtured at a safe distance.

Chapter XV in which I grapple with democracy

The world in 2016 resembled a volcano which had been heating up beneath the surface and then erupted with populism, radicalism and corruption pouring over the prevailing establishment.

In Russia, while the economy was contracting for the second year in a row and the standard of living was falling, the government remained stubbornly preoccupied with foreign policy. In 2015, Russia spent $66.4 billion on defence, making it the fourth largest military spender behind the US, China and Saudi Arabia. Russian troops were being regularly exercised at home, but also abroad, in Syria.

According to a July 2016 survey, two thirds of Russians thought that the US presented a threat to world peace. Over half of the respondents believed that Russia ought to re-establish its authority in the global political arena. The hostility of the West towards Russia had been drilled into the minds of ordinary Russians. Pacifists had been labelled as national traitors, bankrolled by the US.

In an increasingly jittery world, the 2016 NATO summit authorised the stationing of 4,000 (mostly American) combatants in the Baltic States and in Poland, precariously close to the Russian border. An accident, a sudden action by a single fanatic or a deliberate provocation might easily result in hostilities on a terrifying scale. The West had been running its own propaganda, cultivating an image of Russia as an aggressor and thereby putting the world at risk of a new world war.

London, June 2016

On June 24th 2016, I woke up just before 5am. Light was already streaming through the curtains, and a resident blackbird was marking its territory with an elaborate tune. Later it occurred to me that its song was the only sane, reassuring thing that ghastly morning. Still half-asleep, I found a remote control and switched on the radio. It was the morning after the referendum in which British citizens voted on whether to leave the European Union. The news reader was reporting the numbers of voters by constituency, commenting on the high voter turnout, which amounted to 72% nationwide. The tone of her voice was unusually sombre, with a hint of real sadness. I bolted from my bed and ran into the living room to switch on the TV. I learned that 52% of Britons, the required simple majority, had voted to leave the EU.

I experienced all the classic stages of grief: disbelief, anger, bargaining, depression and finally – acceptance. The British people whom I had always regarded as rational and pragmatic, rather than emotional or sentimental, had voted to restore their full sovereignty. They had been swayed by a lost sense of identity and belonging, and a romantic idea of post-imperial nostalgia. They voted to get rid of the bureaucratic shackles of the EU, but no one I spoke to could quite pinpoint the actual hindrance to their daily lives caused by EU laws and regulations. Eventually I realised that the vote was swung not by the comfortably off, romantically inclined voters but by the disenfranchised people, who were fed up with the Westminster government and its divisive policies. These people, who, if pressed upon, had no real axe to grind with the EU, wanted to be heard by the political elite, who had become so estranged from the very people they were supposed to represent, that when the voters had their say, democracy made sure their voices were heard loud and strong.

When David Cameron announced his resignation as Prime Minister; when Jeremy Corbyn, the opposition leader, lost the support of the Labour parliamentarians; when the British pound plummeted against the dollar and the markets ran amok amidst all the uncertainty, it seemed to me that Great Britain, the eternal pillar of sense and sensibility, had crumbled. It was ironic that the island I had chosen as my refuge from the incessant unpredictability of Russia found itself in such a predicament.

My mind travelled back to 1991 when, at the age of eleven, I had witnessed the collapse of the Soviet Union. There had been no referendum, no democratic vote, yet in the feverish days of the attempted August 1991 coup d'état, which is what ultimately caused the USSR to disband, Russian liberals found themselves on the streets of Moscow, protesting against the culprits. That time is remembered as the only period in recent history when the words "freedom", "democracy" and "opposition" meant something tangible to Russians. At the same time, plenty of hardcore communists wished for the return of the old days of stability, state prices and the ideological supremacy of Leninism, however unrealistic their aspirations were. The liberal and the communist camps had little overlap and didn't sympathise with each other. Boris Yeltsin dealt a fatal blow to the plotters and didn't shy away from his victory. He swiftly marginalised Mikhail Gorbachev, and by the end of that year, the USSR was dissolved. Turbulent times followed, not because of the political uncertainty but because in Russia and in the former Soviet Republics there were no institutions, no laws and no law-enforcement system to pave out the smooth transition to the new world order.

After Gorbachev's half-hearted reforms, Yeltsin's economic team was much more decisive. The state control of prices was abolished in January 1992, and in that month alone prices increased on average by 245%. To put this in perspective, when we returned to St. Petersburg after the cruise on the Baltic Sea in early January, my parents thought they had enough roubles to spend a night in a hotel and to buy flights back to Ekaterinburg. In fact, they were only able to pay for a meal. I was just a child, and probably still high on the bananas I had gorged during my first trip abroad. But my parents and all their contemporaries, lived through seismic changes which they simply had to take on the chin. In fact, many thrived in the uncertainty of the early 1990s, and entrepreneurship flourished. Foreign investment poured into Russia. Changes happened at the speed of light. Looking back at those times with the benefit of hindsight, that lawlessness and the lack of institutional accountability elevated some to unimaginable riches and pushed many into poverty and despair. Contemplating the collapse of the Soviet Union today reveals that while the wounds of the sudden severance healed quickly, the scar tissue stayed and has been the source of a dull, recurring ache for Russians ever since.

The older generation especially regretted the collapse of the Soviet Union and struggled to find solace in the decades that followed. In 2015 I listened to old men and women in Russia, Ukraine and Georgia, letting them talk and vent their frustrations. Previously I would have jumped in and explained to them that the command economy had been unsustainable, that the Soviet Union had lived beyond its means and that the restructuring had been necessary. I'd tell them that it was the government's fault that social justice wasn't the priority in Moscow, Kiev or Tbilisi. I'd argue that Russian oil and gas revenues of the boom years weren't invested in infrastructure to support other industries, or spent on healthcare, science and education.

This time I stayed silent and learned about their pensions, which barely covered their rent and did not stretch far enough to pay for food and medical expenses. I watched them sell sunflower seeds, homemade pickles and jams outside metro stations. I absorbed their sense of great sadness and disappointment. These people had survived the Great Patriotic War, they had fought, worked in factories and they had believed in the Soviet Union. They had lived for the big idea of communist supremacy, they were proud of their nation's achievements in industrialisation, science, technology and sports. They thought of themselves – Russians, Ukrainians, Georgians – as brothers and sisters. Today they are struggling to hang on to the idea that their lives weren't meaningless.

The younger generation wants to live rather than struggle. They feel that in the past Russians overdosed on big ideas. They live in a different Russia, drink German beer, shop at IKEA and support Liverpool. They go on holiday to Turkey, Egypt, Sochi or the Crimea, concerned only with the cost and the facilities, not the political agenda of their choices. Top and middle managers in Moscow earn more than their Western counterparts. They enjoy the power of money and rather than let the past dictate their future, they make the most of today.

Turning my mind back to Britain, I realised, of course, that its economy would endure the temporary turbulence and pull through. Unlike Russia, Britain has powerful legislative bodies, strong institutions, a robust infrastructure, and it offers support and incentives to grass-roots businesses. Entrepreneurs thrive in uncertainty. The economy will cope, but the social implications may persist. I watched in disbelief the news about hate crime being on the rise, ministers failing to deal with the political uncertainty and the widespread bitterness. Democracy had triumphed, but what was there to celebrate?

I thought of the forthcoming parliamentary elections in Russia in September 2016. I had wanted to urge my friends and family to vote against the ruling party, to make their voices heard, to let democracy show the Kremlin insiders that people were fed up with kleptocracy and lawlessness, the government's focus on foreign policy at the expense of social justice and economic instability, which would prevail for as long as Russia relied on the cyclical oil and gas exports. It was high time for the ordinary people of Russia to show the elite that its job was not to look after a handful of oligarchs but to represent the one hundred and forty million people from Kaliningrad to Vladivostok.

Now I was no longer sure. Would the turmoil be worth it? Haven't Russians had enough? The general public had learned to stay away from politics, and most of my friends told me they simply focussed on work, family, holidays and personal ambitions. When I asked a friend from Kamchatka what he thought about the current situation in Russia and its future, he wrote back saying: "Have you been drinking?"

***

Ekaterinburg, July 2016

It is summer and time for my annual pilgrimage to Ekaterinburg. After a tremulous month in the UK, I am heading to Russia for peace and tranquillity. Homesickness builds up gradually as I pause by the photo of my late grandmother, Baba Tonya, before I sit down to write. On an unusually sultry day in London I develop a craving for *okroshka*, the summer soup. I suddenly feel the urge to read a book in Russian and race to Waterstone's on Piccadilly, only to find nothing quite suitable in the specialist section of the stiflingly hot store. At a Russian food shop, I buy a handful of Bird's Milk chocolates, which taste impossibly sweet, but help to indulge my nostalgia. At night, as I drift into sleep, I conjure up an image of the *dacha*, of my mum kneeling by her vegetable patch, and Roxy, an ageing German shepherd with sorrowful eyes, who never fails to recognise me and rolls over on her side, inviting me to pat her skinny belly. By the day of my departure, the image of home in my head is exquisite in its painstaking detail: the smell of a bundle of birch twigs in my parents' *banya* (Russian sauna), the refreshing crunch of cucumbers from Mum's greenhouse, the dark stains on my fingers from picking wild blueberries, and the ominous sound of a cuckoo. My superstitious grandmother used to ask the cuckoo "How long will I live?" and count its calls.

At last I pack some presents and head to the airport. I love flying, perhaps because being on a plane above the clouds and the labels people give each other liberates me from the need to belong. In Britain I will never conform to the national character or recognise a nursery rhyme I didn't grow up with. I will always be an immigrant. In Russia they now see a foreigner in me too: I dress, behave and think differently. They say I speak with a Baltic accent, just like Barbara Brylska, who starred in the beloved New Year's Eve comedy *The Irony of Fate*. I laugh at the comparison but inwardly I know they are right: living abroad has changed me too much to feel at home in Russia. Being on the road is my happy place now.

Back in the booming days of the early noughties it was possible to fly to Ekaterinburg directly from London with British Airways, but now I always fly via Moscow. At the boarding gate at Heathrow airport I appraise my fellow travellers: a few London businessmen are flying Economy and look a little unsettled. Given the amount of scaremongering in the British press, it is not altogether surprising. One man is holding a red hardcover, *2017 War with Russia: An urgent warning from senior military command* – I truly hope it's fiction. Most travellers look Russian. There are a few bored youths, absorbed in their gadgets, a number of well-dressed mothers taking their young children to see grandparents in Russia and a great many homeward-bound Muscovites with bulging Duty Free shopping bags. If there is a recession in Russia, these people are immune to it. Business Class is full of mostly overweight men and somewhat malnourished but beautifully presented women, sipping champagne.

I take my seat and notice that the man next to me is

reading Mikhail Gorbachev's latest book *The New Russia*.

"Do you like it?" I cannot resist asking.

"I've only just started reading it," he replies. "A great man."

"That's not what Russians think…"

"Oh?"

"Some Russians blame him for the collapse of the Soviet Union, and others think he wasn't strong enough to see *perestroika* through. He kept changing tack. He tried to appease the Communists and yet he wanted capitalism. And he cared too much about his image in the West. You clapped him, Russians booed him off."

We talk a little longer but then I turn to my book. I am reading Svetlana Alexievich, the Nobel-prize-winning Belorussian author who has written a series of books, which are best described as the missing history of Russia. She records true stories about Soviet women who fought in the Second World War, about the victims of the Chernobyl disaster, the young men who perished in the USSR war with Afghanistan and the controversial 1990s when people lost jobs, stability and their identity as Soviet citizens. Alexievich writes about tectonic events yet she reduces them to human scale. Love, death, good and evil are the main characters of her books. I feel sick as I read: it's painless to remember the 1988 war between Armenia and Azerbaijan as it was reported on the news, but it's quite another thing to read about an Armenian girl being raped, skinned and beaten to death in Baku while at the very same time entire Azeri families were burnt alive in an Armenian village near Erevan. Like most Russians, until the Nobel Prize award I had never even heard of Alexievich, who, as it turns out, has been writing and publishing her books in Russian since 1985.

In Moscow I don't have to wait long for my next flight and, holding on to the rail of a bus which is taking passengers to the plane, I look around to see whether I might recognise anyone from Ekaterinburg. It is naive and fruitless, of course, but I convince myself that there is something vaguely familiar in the faces around me. The travellers to Ekaterinburg look less glamorous than the passengers on my earlier flight; most of them are heading to the Urals for business, judging by their suits and briefcases. Everyone looks sombre, Russians usually do. They say it's because in our culture "laughing without a reason means you are an idiot", according to a popular proverb, but I am inclined to blame their grim faces on the early hour and the irritating drizzle outside. Two hours later, we land in Ekaterinburg and inevitably, my pulse quickens, and I rush off the plane with irrational urgency given that I still have to wait for my luggage.

I spot my mother at arrivals just before she sees me and waves with a colourful bunch of flowers she must have picked from her garden. My parents have always met me with flowers: roses bought from the overpriced airport stall, peonies or asters from auntie Natasha's prized flowerbed. In the split second before our eyes meet, I gently stop the clock and look closely at my mother. The tall, bold woman who used to turn heads is no more. My mother has wilted like a flower in a vase of stale water. Her shoulders are stooped, her entire frame has shrunk somehow, and presently she is overshadowed by a sign reading "Sberbank", held up by a taxi driver who is waiting for his passenger beside her. She does not smile, and

I cannot quite decipher her expression: it's not sorrow or anxiety, but a look of resignation, devoid of any joy. And then I notice something else. My mum's stature now resembles that of her mother, Baba Tonya, and I recognise in her face my grandmother's look of uncertainty. I feel a surge of love, I grin and shout: "Mama!" She smiles too, her face now flooded with unreserved happiness, and we hug each other tightly.

Over the last ten years or so, Mum and I have become increasingly close. Unlike my father, she never weighed me down with expectations and if in private she longed for grandchildren and regretted my living so far away, she never showed it. She came to visit me in London once a year and let me drag her to Embankment to cheer on London Marathon runners in the rain or to an obscure hippy hangout in Ladbroke Grove to sample ridiculously overpriced vegan fare in a cramped pop-up joint. When I was working in the City, she was content to see me only on weekends, walking by herself in Hyde Park and spending nights on her own in my empty flat. When I ran the London Marathon myself, she braved the crowds to meet me at the finish line and then filled my bath with ice, however crazy the feat itself or the recommended remedy appeared to her. She never reproached me for quitting my job to go travelling or to pursue my quest for fulfilment. She simply listened and let me indulge in the dreams I stubbornly followed. She worried about my writing about Putin or travelling to Kiev in turbulent times, but she knew better than to try and stop me. Whatever disappointments and pain she encountered in her own life, she resolved to help me celebrate my journey with the words I'll never forget: "I'm with you!"

Now we leave the airport and call my father, who is waiting outside the parking lot to save the extortionate fee. He comes quickly and helps me with my suitcase. We are cordial to each other. It is not in my nature to bite my tongue, but I've learned over the years to do just that in the company of my father. Any mention of politics would cause a fight. I use tiredness as an excuse to spend much of the journey home listening to the radio rather than talking. I gaze around looking for posters of the parliamentary election campaign. I have heard that the ruling party, United Russia, had come up with a sinister slogan, *"Vazhno Vybrat' Pravil'no" (It's vital to choose correctly)*. The *correct* choice is naturally *Vladimir Vladimirovich Putin*, and the three words conveniently abbreviate to the same acronym: *VVP*. Strangely, there are no posters at the sides of the motorway or anywhere in the city. It's as if campaigning is pointless: both the insiders and the opposition know very well who is going to win.

At the *dacha* I am first greeted by Roxy, who licks my face, and her imbecile son Toby, who nearly knocks me down. The *dacha*, shielded by pine trees and guarded by woodpeckers, is a welcome oasis, at least until my father turns on the TV. I go to the garden to find my ninety-year-old grandmother, Baba Lena, sitting under an umbrella; her swollen feet are resting on a plastic chair in front of her. She is tackling a crossword, her weekly challenge. She struggles to walk and complains about a multitude of ailments, but she reads a book in two days, keeps up-to-date with the news and takes a particular pleasure in tracing my frequent travels in her old atlas. We greet each other warmly. Just then auntie Natasha appears from around the corner with an enormous bunch of rhubarb and a flashing smile. True to herself, she is wearing a bright red lipstick while pottering around her garden. It's only when I ask about uncle Borya that her smile fades.

Uncle Borya was diagnosed with Alzheimer's in 2010, when he was sixty-one years old. By that time the disease had already wreaked havoc: uncle Borya had become increasingly forgetful, sometimes confused and often irritable. He was forced into early retirement from the university and deteriorated rapidly. One time, auntie Natasha lost him on the way back home from the supermarket, and she didn't track him down until the next day. He was sitting on a bench not far from their block of flats, helplessly staring into space. Another time when they were returning to Ekaterinburg from the *dacha* he stepped off the train one station early when auntie Natasha had dozed off. He went missing, and the incident was even reported in the local papers, until two days later a tram driver reported a strange, disoriented man to the police. As if early-onset of Alzheimer's wasn't tragic enough, uncle Borya's illness wasn't perceived as such in my family. Baba Lena, his mother-in-law, was especially unforgiving about his forgetfulness and was constantly grumbling about him. In her eyes, he was good-for-nothing and a nuisance. Others too found it hard to be compassionate. It shocked me, and we argued about it, but it wasn't altogether surprising, with mental illness still being very much a subject of stigma in Russia. Prejudices remain unchallenged and the vast majority of people with depression, Alzheimer's, bipolar disorder and other mental illnesses receive no support and no treatment.

Boris Borisovich Bagirov, my uncle Borya, a respected academic and a popular professor of philosophy and political science, who had wooed his future wife by singing arias and who had challenged me with philosophical riddles every summer, became a shadow of his former self. Last summer he was often found in the garden, picking and eating redcurrants. His movements were methodical but his gaze was vacant. When I greeted him, he would nod and smile, but he didn't recognise me. I would look him in the eyes, which were still kind but no longer inquisitive. I would say something, desperate to get through to him, but he would avert his gaze. I gave auntie Natasha some money so that she could afford to leave her husband at a private hospital for a week or so and have some rest. This year, she tells me, uncle Borya is staying at the hospital for the entire summer. I can be as indignant as I like about the prejudices of my family, but it is not me who has to wash the incontinent man every morning and provide round-the-clock care. I am glad when mum calls me and I leave my aunt and my grandmother, refusing to believe that one day, sickness and old age will catch up with me too.

It is time to pay my respects to my mum's vegetable garden. It's hard to believe that once upon a time she showed no interest in gardening and ridiculed her sister-in-law for being so obsessed with her cabbage patch or her exotic flowerbeds. Mum has changed into shorts and a vest and leads me to her plantation. I feel like a foreign dignitary asked to judge a gardening competition, but of course I cannot afford to give anything other than top marks. The patch is enormous, and almost half of it is devoted to potatoes, an essential Russian staple. Then there are neat rows of carrots, beetroots, all kinds of cabbages, fragrant herbs, boisterous peas and garden berries; the greenhouse is bursting with cucumbers, sweet peppers and tomatoes. Inside it smells luxuriously of basil. We inspect the garden row by row, bush by bush, plant by plant, and I inhale pride and joy. This is mum's domain, and I can see that this garden is her subsistence and her salvation, something more important and tangible than words or prayers can ever be.

That evening our dinner is a feast, marking the return of the prodigal daughter, or so my father jokes. There is pickled herring served with onion and boiled new potatoes. Mum opens a tin of *malosolnye ogurtsy*, cucumbers in light brine which retain their crunch and fresh green colour. She preserved them herself. There is a big salad of tomatoes, radishes, cucumbers and dill, traditionally dressed with *smetana,* thick sour cream. My father has smoked a large trout, using the same method that his father taught him years ago. Auntie Natasha has brought us a pair of taut, shiny aubergines from her greenhouse and mum makes a grilled aubergine caviar heaped with fresh coriander, basil and parsley. There is *charlotka*, my family's favourite apple pie, for pudding.

I have so many questions. Where is Russia heading? Who are you going to vote for in the September elections? How can you watch those ridiculous interior design programmes featuring tasteless palaces of Moscow oligarchs or the angry talk shows? But I am not about to spoil a family meal. I sense that my mother and my aunt, like many Russians, simply don't want to talk about current affairs, because the truth would be too painful to accept. I ask my father not to turn on the TV while we eat and he obliges. Afterwards, when he insists on watching the 9 o'clock news, I persuade Mum to walk with me to the lake, as otherwise she sees nothing but her stove and her garden. There, on a generously warm summer night, we take in the splendour of the Volchikhinskoe reservoir. When a fast train passes by, we wave to the driver and he blows the horn, just like we did thirty years ago.

***

A couple of days later, I am heading to Ekaterinburg on a suburban train. I understand why people back in Britain feel baffled by the overwhelming popularity of Putin and are alarmed by the Kremlin's aggressive international politics. The two go hand-in-hand: the elevated sense of collective might offers Russians a welcome relief from their daily struggles, and the confident image of Putin, when he appears with Western leaders on television, translates into high approval ratings. The people I see on the train got up at dawn and headed into the forest to pick wild blueberries, lingonberries and mushrooms. Now they are returning to Ekaterinburg to sell their pickings. Others are heading into town just for a day to get prescription drugs and buy food staples at large supermarkets. These people don't have cars, otherwise they would not be using the train. They live from one day to the next, regardless of whether the leader is Brezhnev, Gorbachev or Putin at the helm. A dollop of national pride, peppered with the Great Patriotic War songs and images, goes a long way to soothing these people's woes.

For people born in the Soviet Union, it is impossible not to think back to the days when their motherland took up nearly half the world map or to forget what it took to defeat Hitler. Today nationalism is sprouting not just in Russia but in

Britain. Both countries are intoxicated with ideas of greatness and power. And both elevate the US to the status of a special nation. In Russia, the US is cultivated as a special enemy; in Britain, it is considered a special friend. The Americans, by contrast, have long diversified their interests and influence too much to pick out any particular friend or foe as "special".

I was born in the USSR, but I no longer have a Russian worldview. I belong to the tribe of "achievers", who did well at school, went away to university, climbed a professional ladder and benefited from social and geographic mobility. Conversely, people with "ascribed" identities – as sociologists call it – derive their worldview from the milieu they come from. Most Russians live in the same place where they were born. More than 60% of Brits still live within 20 miles of where they lived aged fourteen. Many of these people are discombobulated by mass immigration and the social change, brought about by globalisation and the new mobility of the labour force. I want Russia to change, to become more democratic, to have a well diversified economy and a fairer society. I want Russia to co-operate with other countries, not to train its own people to hate and blame others for the country's woes. And of course I voted to remain in the European Union, because I am a cosmopolitan citizen who views the world as one big interconnected place.

***

My self-righteous reverie is interrupted by our arrival at Ekaterinburg's main railway station. It is a major hub with a baroque-style building, recently renovated and painted in an unlikely shade of lime yellow, which reminds me of the colour of the dress Queen Elizabeth II wore for her ninetieth birthday celebration earlier this year. The station square is buzzing with people – migrant workers coming from Tajikistan, foreign backpackers stepping off the Transsiberian train, Mormons with badges bearing their names in Russian and locals heading for their *dachas*. I make my way to the metro station, which by some hapless design is located a few minutes' walk away behind the railway station. Ekaterinburg's metro is apparently the shortest underground line in the world, and it might hold another record: the longest period of construction. Work began in 1980 and the first four stops opened in the 1990s. The fifth stop by my late grandmother's house was finally opened at the end of 2002, but Baba Tonya didn't live to see it. It takes just a few minutes to get to her former house from the railway station and I come out slowly, taking my time to adjust to the unfamiliar surroundings.

My beloved circus building is still there, but it is now overshadowed by new corporate high-rises. An impromptu antique market has mushroomed by the station, with *babushkas* selling bric-a-brac. My grandmother's old house looks shabby. The benches where she and her neighbours used to sit after their afternoon strolls have disappeared. The old Fruit & Vegetable store has been replaced by a soulless flower boutique. I realise that it is silly to feel disappointed.

I reach the church, hidden by poplar trees, where my grandmother's burial service took place. The building has been renovated. The adjacent Novo-Tikhvinsky convent, dating back to the beginning of the eighteenth century, but closed by the Soviets in 1920, is being restored. The new building looks ambitiously large. It seems funding isn't a problem for Orthodox churches. Just as in Moscow, where in 2010 Patriarch Kirill, the Russian Orthodox bishop, announced plans to build 200 new churches in the capital's suburbs, in Ekaterinburg, ideological expansion is also underway. As I walk towards the Sports Palace, where as a child I practised artistic gymnastics, I pass the ruins of a former hospital building. A cardiological centre nearby is still standing, but it's in a terrible state of disrepair. I recall a recent conversation with my old classmate Ksenia, who told me that the ambulance had refused to take her 86-year-old grandfather to the hospital because of his age. The dressed-up version of homecoming I had played in my mind a week ago has now been thoroughly washed, rinsed and tumble-dried.

I take a tram to *Plotinka* (little dam), the centre of Ekaterinburg, which, unlike the city's nooks and crannies, has been well looked after. The promenade by the pond and the opening vista look magnificent. Bright flowers are planted everywhere, something I don't recall seeing since Soviet days. Young *eburzhata* (an affectionate name for the citizens of Ekaterinburg which rhymes with the word "little bears") meet their dates and stroll by the pond, smiling and taking photos. I walk to the recently opened Yeltsin Centre, a museum of Russian history and a cultural hub, and marvel at how modern it is, with services and facilities to compete with the world's best museums. I travel through the history of the Soviet Union since the Bolshevik revolution, through the Civil War, the hardship of the 1920s followed by the ascent of Stalin, the terror of the repressions, the Great Patriotic War, which was followed by more repressions and exiles. In total, 50 million people went through the *Gulag* (Soviet forced labour camps) and 5 million more were exiled.

Upstairs the exhibition shows the decade of Yeltsin's presidency with scrupulous honesty – something I simply did not expect to see in Russia today. In the section dedicated to the Chechen Wars, I find a handful of emotional essays, hand-written by Chechen children, entitled "How I Spent the War", replacing the traditional September essay on the bliss of summer holidays. My favourite part of the exhibition is a short video projected on a large screen where famous Russian personalities summarise the main principles of the 1993 Constitution of Russia, something Yeltsin had bitterly fought against the Duma in order to pass. The voices on the screen declare that Russian citizens have rights to free speech, organisation of marches and demonstrations, and secrecy of private communication. The Russian Constitution explicitly forbids propaganda and censorship. It places human rights and individual freedoms above everything else.

I stay in the museum for hours, then eventually I walk back to Lenin Street, Ekaterinburg's main avenue. In fact, it was renamed Main Avenue in early 1990s, but the Soviet name stuck. Anya and her husband moved here recently. I find my childhood friend, as always, in the kitchen, where she is preparing a feast for her son's tenth birthday. Anya is on her second maternity leave and it's the first time I meet her newly born daughter, who is the spitting image of her mother. Anya tells me about their summer holiday in Crimea and makes me a pot of tea with local herbs she brought back. We concentrate on discussing Crimean caves and castles, the shamelessly overpriced watermelons and the medicinal properties of Crimean herbal tea.

I leave reluctantly but I have an important appointment to keep. It is our twentieth school graduation anniversary, and our first reunion. It's remarkable how little my classmates have changed from their seventeen-year-old selves. I recognise the same smiles, postures and mannerisms. In other ways time has left its imprint. Everyone gathered around the table is married. Some have even been married twice. Everyone has children, some as many as three. What's strange, perhaps, is that some women are stay-at-home mums – it's common enough in the West, but this is the first generation of housewives in Russia. Still, most women have full-time jobs: Olga is an economist, Masha is an architect, and Lena runs her own construction business. Tentatively at first, we begin to share stories.

Lyuba is telling us about her recent vacation in Norway. She could not believe the number of Muslims they saw in "the very centre" of Oslo. "It's as if they've taken over", she said, "imagine what it's doing to the European culture. France and Germany too are flooded with Africans these days."

"When I come to Paris, I want croissants and fashion boutiques," agrees Dima. "When Pavel – do you remember him? – married an Indian girl, I was OK with that in principle, but I don't want European culture to be diluted with peanuts and hijabs."

Someone else remembers a thirteen-year-old Russian-German girl raped by a gang of Syrians. I quickly tell them that story was a hoax, the girl later told the police she had made it all up, but I bet the Russian networks "forgot" to report it. I excuse myself and run for the restroom.

When I return, Zhenya, the son of my former paediatrician Ludmila Sergeevna, is showing photos of his kids and talking about his obsession with cycling. I'm grateful for the change of subject. We've not seen each other for so long that I'd rather reminisce about our school days or catch up on their lives since, than lecture them on ethics. But this year politics forces its way into dinner conversations, trumping all other subjects. Vika, who teaches jurisprudence, asks me about Brexit and I tell her about the vote.

"The EU became the scapegoat, responsible for all the problems in Britain, like underfunded national healthcare and education," I say.

"Like some people here blame the US and Western sanctions for rising prices and unemployment," she nods.

"Well, they say the British people have spoken and made their voices heard. We have a new Prime Minister now and the opposition party has been shaken up as well. You too have elections coming up…"

"Yes," says Vika, "but you know how it goes here."

"You could vote and yes, they may rig the results, but you can't just do nothing and hope for the best. Russia is still a democratic republic, that's what the Constitution says, right?" I say, conveniently holding up a slim but precious booklet I picked up at the museum.

"Democracy… Yes, we have our own special version of it, and what people really want is a strict, benevolent tsar," says Vika.

"All we know from history," I say, "is that Russia played at being a constitutional monarchy for about five minutes before turning into a communist state virtually overnight.

We've been trying to become a democracy since the fall of the Soviet Union, but under Putin we've been moving backwards because of all the lies being fed to people. Forget democracy, what we need is truth."

"Yanka, what are you arguing about?" interrupts Lyesha, "The truth is – your glass is empty! What are you drinking?"

I don't protest, and finally politics is swept aside. We remember our school days when we all thought of ourselves as terribly grown-up. There is a shared sense of gratitude to our teachers who sheltered us from the erratic world outside school. Today everyone looks relaxed and happy in their own skin, even if, as I feel, I am only just beginning the journey of self-discovery. It is strange that after a day of wandering through the city that I no longer recognise as my own, I do feel at home in the company of my former classmates. We've not kept in touch and have only recently re-connected thanks to social media, yet everyone seems at ease. When Olga tells me she had always known that one day I'd become a writer, I bask in the happiness of being so well understood. It's a fleeting homecoming, which is what makes it possible to pick the choicest morsels, like the legacy of old friendships, and appreciate them for what they are.

I find myself returning to London with my nostrils filled with the scent of fresh pinewood and a tentative feeling of optimism. It's places like the Yeltsin Centre in Ekaterinburg and the image of my mother enjoying the book by Svetlana Alexievich that I bought for her that give me hope. When I doze off on the plane, the lines written by the nineteenth-century Russian poet Feodor Tutchev come to my mind:

Russia cannot be understood with mere intellect
Or measured by a common yardstick.
Russia is so special
That you can only believe in it.

Acknowledgments

I am forever indebted to my friend and mentor David Frank who persuaded me to write up my story and supported me every step of the way.

It is equally impossible to imagine this book taking shape without the encouraging, earnest and invaluable help from Charlotte Seymour, who believed in me from day one. Her comments and advice spurred me on, and I am immensely grateful for her friendship and guidance. Both David and Charlotte have patiently corrected every wrong article and inserted the missing ones, overlooking my Russian tendency to skip them.

A special thank you goes to Simon Kuper who, in addition to being one of the most thought-provoking journalists on the planet, found time to help me with advice, to read and edit my memoir and to show me what it really means to be generous.

Alexandra Burda has created the most beautiful cover for *Bird's Milk*, teaching herself the mastery of traditional Russian art of Gzhel in the process. It was at that moment when I saw the first draft of the cover that I finally believed that my book was coming to life. I'm incredibly lucky to have found such a talented artist.

I am hugely grateful to everyone who has helped me remember all the lively anecdotes of the past 35 years and of course to those who have filled my life with colourful memories in the first place. I am truly indebted to all my teachers, especially Elena Aleksandrovna Krasovskaya, my English teacher in Ekaterinburg, for inspiring and challenging me at school.

I am also grateful to Jonnie Goodwin, who allowed me the flexibility I needed to support myself with freelance work while writing this book.

Above all, I owe most to my parents, Tatiana and Sergey Bakunin. Without the discipline instilled in me from childhood and the education they helped me receive, I would not have had the audacity or the diligence to fulfil my dream: write and publish a book.

ABOUT THE AUTHOR

Jana Bakunina was born in Ekaterinburg, Russia's fourth largest city, situated nearly 2,000km east of Moscow. At 16, she won a scholarship to a boarding school in Germany and from there secured a place to study Economics & Management at Oxford. She moved to London to work in the City, and after a career in investment banking and the media, she turned to writing.

Jana Bakunina currently works as a freelance journalist and is consulting businesses on corporate finance. She has been published by *New Statesman*, *The Spectator* and *Huffington Post*. She has a weekly column in a Russian language paper *Pulse UK* and writes for www.lifetonic.co.uk, a blog about life skills, entrepreneurship and personal development. Her interviews with inspiring women are published on www.ladieswhoimpress.com.